William Ansell Day

The Pythouse Papers

Correspondence Concerning the Civil War, the Popish Plot, And a Contested

Election in 1680

William Ansell Day

The Pythouse Papers
Correspondence Concerning the Civil War, the Popish Plot, And a Contested Election in 1680

ISBN/EAN: 9783744691871

Printed in Europe, USA, Canada, Australia, Japan

Cover: Foto ©ninafisch / pixelio.de

More available books at **www.hansebooks.com**

The Pythouse Papers.

The Pythouse Papers:

CORRESPONDENCE

CONCERNING THE CIVIL WAR,

THE POPISH PLOT, AND

A CONTESTED ELECTION IN 1680.

Transcribed from MSS. in the possession of
V. F. BENETT-STANFORD, Esq., M.P.

Edited, and with an Introduction, by
WILLIAM ANSELL DAY,
AUTHOR OF "THE RUSSIAN GOVERNMENT IN POLAND."

LONDON:
BICKERS & SON, 1, LEICESTER SQUARE.
1879.

WYMAN AND SONS, PRINTERS,
GREAT QUEEN STREET, LINCOLN'S INN FIELDS,
LONDON, W.C.

CONTENTS.

		PAGE
INTRODUCTION		1
LETTERS:—		

1.	The King to Prince Rupert	3 Feb. 1643 ...	1
2.	Same to „	4 Nov. 1643 ...	1
3.	Same to „	12 Nov. 1643 ...	2
4.	Same to „	4 Mar. 1644 ...	3
5.	Same to „	12 Mar. 1643 ...	4
6.	Same to „	15 Mar. 1643 ...	5
7.	Same to „	27 Mar. 1643 ...	5
8.	Same to „	21 April 1644 ...	6
9.	Same to „	24 April 1644 ...	7
10.	Lord Grandison to Prince Rupert ...	8 Feb. 1643 ...	8
11.	Henry Hastings [Lord Loughborough] to the King	15 Jany. [1644]...	9
12.	Earl of Derby to Prince Rupert... ...	... ...	10
13.	Duke of Richmond to „ ...	21 April [ ]...	10
14.	Sir Arthur Aston to „ ...	22 Jan. [ ]...	12
15.	Ferdinando, Earl of Huntingdon, to Sir Edward Nicholas	... [ ]	13
16.	Sir William Vavasour to Prince Rupert ...	[1643]	15
17.	Duke of Richmond to „ ...	18 Sept. [1643]...	16
18.	Same to „ ...	Nov. 1643 ...	17
19.	Same to „ ...	25 March [1644]	18
20.	Duke of Newcastle to „ ...	1 July, 1644 ...	19
21.	Sir Jacob Astley to „ ...	12 Jan. 1645 ...	20
22.	Lord Ethyn [General King] to „ ...	23 Jan. 1645 ...	21
23.	J. O. Grandison to „ ...	7 Feb. 1645 ...	22
24.	Ralph Goodwin to „ ...	7 Feb. 1645 ...	23
25.	Colonel [Sir Samuel] Tuke to Major-General Porter	... ...	24

			PAGE
26.	Daniel O'Neille to Prince Rupert	...	25
27.	Finding of the King in Council of War on Surrender of Bristol	21 Oct. 1645	25
28.	Anonymous Letter to Prince Rupert	[1645]	27
29.	Henry Osborne to ,,	1 Nov. 1645	28
30.	Sir Edward Nicholas to Prince Rupert	7 Dec. 1645	29
31.	Petition from Westbury, Wilts, to Sir Thomas Fairfax	28 Feb. 1647	30
32.	Report on Value of Vicarage of Westbury	...	32
33.	Andrew Seymour to ——	16 July, 1647	33
34.	Charles II. to Prince Rupert	18 Dec. [ ]	34
35.	Sir Henry de Vic to Lord ——	7 June, 1653	35
36.	Sir Edw. Nicholas to Prince Rupert	6 Feb. 1656	36
	Letters from Lord Percy	...	39
	Note on Lord Percy	...	41
37.	Lord Percy to Prince Rupert	6 Nov. 1642	45
38.	Same to ,,	[21 Feb. 1643]	47
39.	Same to ,,	[29 April, 1643]	47
40.	Same to ,,	30 [April, 1643]	48
41.	Same to ,,	8 June, [1643]	49
42.	Same to ,,	[3 July, 1643]	50
43.	Same to ,,	6 July, [1643]	50
44.	Same to ,,	...	51
45.	Same to ,,	22 [July, 1643]	53
46.	Same to ,,	23 July, [1643]	54
47.	Same to ,,	29 July, 1643	55
48.	Same to ,,	30 [July, 1643]	56
49.	Same to the King	17 Aug. [1643]	57
50.	Same to Prince Rupert	...	58
51.	Same to ,,	15 Nov. [1643]	59
52.	Same to ,,	21 March, [1644]	60
53.	Same to ,,	28 [March, 1644]	62
54.	Same to ,,	[Same date]	62
55.	Same to ,,	8 July, [1643]	63
56.	The Breviates of the Prince's Letters	...	65

CONTENTS.

Letters from William Benett to his Mother.

57.	31 Jan. 1679	72
58.	10 July, 1679	72
59.	20 Oct. 1679	73
60.	6 Nov. 1679	74

Letters from William Bennett to Colonel Benett.

61.	1 Oct. 1677	80
62.	13 Oct. 1677	81
63.	13 June, 1678	82
64.	7 Jan. 1678	83
65.	31 May, 1679	85
66.	15 Jan. 1680	86
67.	18 Jan. 1680	86
68.	22 Jan. 1680	88
69.	29 Jan. 1680	90
70.	6 Feb. 1680	93
71.	23 Feb. 1680	94
72.	3 March, 1680	96
73.	21 March, 1680	98
74.	No date	100

APPENDIX.

Letter from Lord Shaftesbury to Mr. Bennett... 28 Aug. 1675 ... 102

INTRODUCTION.

THE characters of the men who bore part in the great rebellion stand prominently before us. In the confused chronicles of earlier times the annalist laid on the colours where he chose, he arranged every light and every shade, and with his busy pencil created demi-gods or imagined fiends. In the contest between the King and his disaffected subjects all the conditions were changed; on every side light streams in upon us; the fierce political pamphlets and newspapers of the day, the memoirs, letters, and state papers subsequently published, and the essays at a yet later date of historians, philosophers, and partizans, all contribute to that great store of historical learning on which the inquirer can draw, and from which he may form an estimate of the actors in that eventful strife.

It is difficult, however, to write of the past and not to feel like a partizan, and in almost every essay, memoir, or history we refer to, there are traces of a bitterness of spirit and harshness of judgment which are scarcely consistent with a justly poised balance. No doubt the records of the past history of their own land are of exceptional interest to English writers. In most countries there is a wide gulf between the past and the present; a system of government existed; it became unsuited to the requirements or the will of the nation, and in some political hurricane it was swept away; a new system was erected on the old site, and the very foundations of the former edifice were rooted up—there was no connecting link between them, and though the history of the older structure might have some antiquarian interest it had no real bearing on active political life.

In England, on the contrary, revolutions have in great measure been governed by precedent, and it is natural, where the actions of our ancestors may materially affect our rights, that we should regard them with an interest similar to that which we feel for the politics of our own time, in which history is being enacted before our eyes by the leaders we follow or their antagonists whom we distrust.

It is needless for the purpose of illustrating the letters before us to compose an elaborate essay on their authors—yet their characters are interesting, and a few observations may not be out of place.

Foremost in station, the centre and the mark of all the intrigues and cabals of that stormy epoch, the character of the King is the first subject that commands our attention. Eight generations have lived and passed away since the troubles that beset him commenced, yet his character and career are still the theme on which loyalty delights to dwell and which detraction has made her own. There has been reason alike for panegyric and condemnation; for the exaggerated adulation of the Cavalier, and for the Roundhead's bitter wrath.

No Character in history is better known to us than is this unhappy King. His stately effigy has been handed down to us on "the breathing canvass of Vandyke," his noble eloquence, like some costly jewel, has been preserved in the classic setting of Clarendon; and his memory is reverenced by every lover of literature and every student of art. His good resolutions, his noble language, his lofty bearing, his energy and faith commanded the love of his adherents and tardy admiration of his enemies; while the unshrinking steadfastness of his gaze when he had nought save death to look upon, won him back the love of his people, and secured the eventual triumph of his cause.

These qualities and attributes might have formed the basis in another age and under other conditions of a great and magnanimous career. Who does not know however, with what dross the pure metal was alloyed? With tyranny, with irresolution, with fraud; with a fatal tendency to make any and every promise which the exigencies of the hour suggested, and to repudiate them as shamefully, as he had made them rashly the moment pressure was withdrawn. Vacillating, weak, and distrustful of himself, Charles was peculiarly under the influence of those who were about him, and the man who was most unhesitating in his advice and the most confident in insisting upon its adoption, had a prevailing though momentary influence on the wavering Councils of the Crown.

With plans thus perpetually shifting it was impossible for his friends to confide or for his enemies to trust in Charles. The promises made in good faith one day were broken on the next under the influence of some fresh adviser. The plan of an expedition was settled, and almost ere the march was commenced an imperative command withdrew a large portion of the forces engaged in it, thus reducing the remainder to inaction. A treaty was negotiated with the Parliament, and when success was almost attained a letter under the royal hand convicted the writer of prevarication and faithlesness. Thus all was uncertainty in the royal counsels, and irritation gradually hardening into inexorable vengeance in those of his opponents. If we fail to see great faults on either side we wilfully blind ourselves to the truth ; if we fail to discern great virtues we ignore as needlessly some of the brightest characters, and many of the noblest deeds which gem our storm-tossed history.

It must never be forgotten that, as the struggle continued, the Actors in it changed. It was not Hampden and Falkland only who early perished. On every side the ranks of statesman and soldier-patriots were thinned by death or by causes powerful as death itself. There came a time when the haughty integrity of Essex, the chivalry of Waller, "the gentle and generous nature" of Manchester animated no longer the popular armies, when the eloquence of Pym was silenced in the grave, and even Fairfax was regarded with distrust by those whose armies he had led to victory. On the royal side Sir Bevil Grevil fell at Lansdown, and thus was lost the inspiration of his courage, and the spell of his bright example : Northampton died a hero's death on Hopton Heath, and Derby perished on the scaffold.

Gradually from the gloom of the future figure after figure emerged of men once obscure but destined now to fulfil great purposes ; the gloss on the sword of Rebellion had worn off but the weapon retained its temper, and was wielded with unsparing severity and skill. A narrow fanaticism trampled down all trace of chivalrous courtesy, and rested not till it had crushed the cavaliers, and handed over power to a sectarian army and its bigotted but able chief.

Foremost among the Cavaliers—conspicuous by birth, by dauntless courage, which neither policy nor prudence ever checked; by stern resolution, which never wavered before difficulties; by a knowledge of the incidents of war, the marshalling of armies, and the life of camps such as had in those days never been learned in England—Rupert of the Rhine stands conspicuous and alone.

He was cradled in misfortune and nursed in strife. His father, Frederick, Prince Palatine of the Rhine, was the unequal descendant of a long line of illustrious ancestors. Heir to a great position, he might have been the champion and avenger of the Protestant cause, for the opportunity was his if he had had the courage to grasp and the steadfast firmness to hold it. But he was a pedant, a waverer, and a bigot. A brief term of success sufficed to demonstrate his incapacity for rule, and many years of adversity failed to wring from his dull phlegmatic temperament any sentiment more noble than a cold unenterprising patience.

This man was wedded to one of the best and noblest women of her age. The Princess Elizabeth, daughter of James I., had every attribute which can make a woman beloved and reverenced. She had beauty such as few could boast, she had courage none could surpass; she had the pride which well becomes high birth and noble nature, when they are struggling with adversity; and she had a winning and gracious courtesy, which attracted to her the chivalry of England, and earned her the lasting support of the Merchant Princes of Holland. She was popularly known as the "Queen of Hearts," and the name was well bestowed, for, when her fortunes were at the lowest, she received truer and more disinterested homage than crowned Prince or victorious conqueror ever won from hereditary subjects or vanquished foes.

The people of England had fought and prayed for her success. She was sprung from their Royal house; she was fighting the battle of their faith; she had beauty, courage, and long descent; and they rendered her the homage which, under such circumstances, is ever won by unfaltering devotion to a noble cause. The national sympathy, however, outran the sympathy of the Crown; the father and brother of Elizabeth looked coldly on, and gave her husband much advice but little aid; until at length, reft of his dominions, a fugitive and a supplicant, he committed his cause to the champion of his faith, Gustavus of Sweden. The great Swede had, however, many objects to strive for, and many prizes to win. The restoration of the inefficient Frederick to his Electorate could have filled only a small space in the dreams of his far-reaching ambition; and Frederick clung to the robes of his patron a courtier and a pensionary till death terminated his weak and contemptible career.

Rupert was the third son of this ill-fated marriage, and from his earliest youth he had been accustomed to the clang of arms, the march of armies, the perils of the fight, and even the solitude of a dungeon; but the school of arms in which he had been reared was an ill education for a leader in English war.

Sorrowfully, with doubt and hesitation, did the Nobles and Gentlemen of England draw the sword: they were to struggle against kindred and friends; against men who had mingled in the same pursuits, and been animated by the same ends as themselves, and, whichever side was victorious, the strife involved much present suffering and future uncertainty. For what were these risks encountered? On the one part for a King whom no one trusted, and on the other for a Parliament which had become the mouthpiece of faction and the tool of unscrupulous and designing men.

The letter, often quoted, of Sir William Waller to Sir Ralph, afterwards Lord Hopton, expresses in noble language the feeling which prevailed at this moment:—
"My affections to you are so unchangeable, that hostility itself cannot violate my friendship to your person, but I must be true to the cause wherein I serve. The great God, who is the searcher of my heart, knows with what reluctance I go upon this service, and with what perfect hatred I look upon a war without an enemy. The God of peace in his good time send us peace, and in the meantime fit us to receive it! We are both on the stage, and we must act the parts that are assigned to us in this tragedy. Let us do it in a way of honour, and without personal animosities."

The conditions under which Rupert mingled in the struggle were widely different. His only aim was the preservation of his uncle's throne. He risked no great possession; he perilled no vast heritage upon the issue. An exile from his own land, he was little better than an adventurer here; and while he was prepared to devote himself with energy and courage to the Royal cause, his training and antecedents rendered the war he waged sanguinary, wasteful, and licentious.

It was unfortuate for Rupert that he was too early trusted with great command. Although he was used to war, he had not the experience requisite to enable him to conduct an arduous campaign to a victorious close. A brilliant partizan leader, invaluable in a foray or an assault, he would have admirably accomplished the boldest designs of a skilful leader; but his was the hand to execute and not the head to plan. In time, perhaps, his youthful impetuosity and reckless daring might have toned down, and he might have developed the qualities of a great and successful general; but, ere these qualities had time to ripen, the cause he struggled for was lost, monarchy was swept away, and Charles had perished on the scaffold.

Rupert was not 23 years old when the King's Standard was set up at Nottingham in August, 1642, and he came then, at the instance of the Queen, to take the great position of "General of the Horse." He came; thus young, to command men who had seen long service, and a stranger to England, to take a leading part in her civil strife. It is not surprising to find that his energy, decision, and daring soon gave him strong hold on the wavering King. Rupert, ever at hand, trained in arms, always prompt in council and impetuous in the field, was precisely the man to guide Charles. Then, too, it was not unnatural that the dazzling qualities of the Prince should win the admiration and regard of the younger Cavaliers, and, though Statesmen might deprecate his policy, and old soldiers condemn his tactics, he soon had a following of his own—a following which comprised among it some who were dissolute, many who were reckless, but whose every member was animated by the courage, and inspired by the example of their leader.

The first of the letters from the King to Prince Rupert, which is among those now for the first time printed is the letter dated from Oxford, 3rd Feb. 1643 (according to the old style, 1642).

Two days previously the King had written a letter to the Prince stating that at Cirencester and other places "great quantities of cloth canvass and buckram are to be had for supplying the great necessities our soldiers have of suits," and directing him to possess himself of what supplies of this character the army needed, keeping an account of them and giving a ticket to the owners, who were subsequently to "receive such securities for their commodities as they shall have no cause to except against."

Meanwhile arrangements had been made by Lord Hertford and Prince Rupert for an assault upon Cirencester. It was made on the 2nd of February, and after a brief resistance, was successful. The victory was stained by bloodshed and outrage, and Clarendon admits that the town "yielded much plunder, from which the undistinguishing soldiers could not be kept, but was equally injurious to friend and foe; so that many honest men, who were imprisoned by the rebels for not concurring with them, found themselves undone together."*

Whitelock, in his Memorials † says, "A few days afterwards, Prince Rupert, with 4,000 horse and foot, marched by Sudeley Castle to Cirencester: where the magazine of the County lay; this he took, putting the Earl of Stamford's regiment, and many others, to the sword; took 1,100 prisoners, and 3,000 arms."

"These prisoners were led in much triumph to Oxford, where the King and Lords looked on them, and too many smiled at their misery, being tied with cords, almost naked, beaten and driven along like dogs."

This achievement was of great importance to the Royal forces, for it gave them not only the prestige of victory, and the advantage of securing the stores they required, but it also opened up an uninterrupted communication with Worcester and South Wales, a district from which, by the aid of Lord Glamorgan and his father, they confidently reckoned on most important aid.

The letter dated, Oxford 4th November, 1643, speaks of a proposition concerning Lancashire which the King submits to the consideration of the Prince. This proposition was apparently commented on and replied to on the following day, for a letter is inserted in Warburton's Work under the date 6th November, from Mr. Secretary Nicholas to the Prince ‡, in which he replies to "animadversions" the latter had made with regard to the proposed military arrangements, and closes with the following passage:—" Therefore His Majesty

---
* Clarendon, Vol. 3, p. 417, edit. 1826.
† p. 167, edit. 1732.
‡ Rupert & the Cavaliers p. 327, vol. 2.

desires you to send my Lord Byron presently to him, if your Highness can possibly spare him, that this great design may be presently adjusted, for his Majesty thinks it of that weight, that without it not only these countries will be in hazard to be irrevocably lost, but likewise my Lord of Newcastle's army will be put into very great straits as also the Scots are likely to come in with very great disadvantage to the King's service, if this design be not effectually prevented."

No doubt the proposition was, in effect, the plan subsequently adopted—in the first place with complete success, but which finally closed in defeat and ruin—the march to the North, for the purpose of relieving the gallant Countess of Derby, then hard beset in Latham House, and subsequently the attack on the Parliamentary forces under the Earl of Manchester, and the reinforcement of the Royal army, which, under the command of the Marquis of Newcastle, was holding York for the Crown.

On the 12th November, Charles again writes to the Prince, submitting to his judgment the expediency of holding Tossiter (Towcester), and assuring him the report that he was treating for peace was a "damnable ley."

Towcester was at that time of considerable importance, and it does not appear that the suggestion of the King was acted upon, for, a fortnight later, Sir Arthur Aston reports that he is still fortifying the place and preparing provisions according to the Prince's order. The town was at this moment threatened by the Earl of Essex, on behalf of the Parliament, who had formed a depôt at Aylesbury.

With regard to the rumoured negotiation which the King so energetically denied, Whitelocke makes the following remark: "A paper was communicated to both Houses, which was sent from the Prince Harecourt to the Earl of Northumberland, by way of general proposals, for an accommodation between the King and Parliament, and that in the name of the French King, whose Ambassador he was."

Clarendon * states that the Count of Harecourt was sent as an Ambassador Extraordinary from France, with a view to effect a reconciliation between the King and Parliament, and that, the death of Richelieu, and the supremacy of the Queen-Mother and Cardinal Mazarin, led Charles to expect "notable effect from this embassy." It, however, came to nothing.

The letters of the 12th and 15th of March, 164¾ were written at a critical moment. The Irish Regiment of Royalists had been destroyed; the Scottish army had crossed the border and held Sunderland: Sir Thomas Fairfax had defeated Colonel Bellasis at Selby; Lord Derby could no longer "keep Lancashire in reasonable subjection," and the great stronghold of Newark, threatened by Sir John Meldrum, entreated aid from the King.

The importance of this town was evident. If Newark fell, the communication between Oxford and York would be severed, and all the plans of the King deranged. In the meanwhile, everything was wanting, —arms, ammunition, money, and men, so Rupert was despatched into Shropshire with directions to levy what

---

* Vol. 4, p. 325, 329.

forces he could there, and in Chester, and thence to march to the relief of Newark.

This was a hazardous enterprise; but in the loyal Counties of the West men flocked to the banner of the Prince, and, before the enemy had the faintest idea that he had collected any considerable force, he was on his march to encounter them. Clarendon states * that, though the enemy had excellent intelligence, the Prince "was within six miles of them before they believed he thought of them; and charging and routing some of their horse, pursued them with that expedition that he besieged them in their own entrenchments with his horse, before his foot came within four miles. In the consternation, they concluding he must have a vast power and strength to bring them into these straits, he with a number inferior to the enemy, and utterly unaccommodated for an action of time, brought them to accept of leave to depart, that is, to disband without their arms or any carriage or baggage. Thus he relieved Newark, and took about 4,000 arms, 11 pieces of brass cannon, two mortar pieces, and above 50 barrels of powder, which was as unexpected a victory as any happened throughout the war."

With regard to the £400, in a letter from Arthur Trevor to the Prince, dated Oxford, 24th March, 1644, there is the following observation: "Your £400 I am at last raised to a hope of obtaining for you; and when I have it I shall keep the same entire until you please to renew your orders upon me, not knowing what directions have been given by your Highness since your first desiring of that money."†

---

* Vol. 4, p. 444.
† Warburton Vol. 2, p. 387.

After the victory at Newark Rupert returned to Shrewsbury to prepare for his Northern March. It seemed, indeed, that in the North was this great contest to be decided—Lancashire was to be re-won, Latham House to be relieved, and a junction formed with the Marquis of Newcastle, whose forces were threatened with the combined efforts of three distinct armies. Meanwhile all was uncertainty and irresolution at Oxford. Charles shewed physical courage when retreat was impossible and retractation useless; but when he had in difficult circumstances to consider and decide he was always vacillating, weak, and spiritless. He must have known that Rupert required every man he could gather to his banner when he marched into the Northern Counties, yet he wrote the following letters to his Nephew, arresting his progress and crippling his power.

On the 17th of April (the day on which the Queen left him for Exeter) he urges the Prince to advance into the West Riding, and hinder the rebels from advancing northwards, and especially from falling on Newcastle's rear. By another letter, assumed to be of about the same date, he requires Rupert to send 2,000 men to Evesham and march with the remainder of his army wherever he pleases. On the 20th Charles states that, without the assistance he asks of the Prince, he must relinquish those parts of the West where Rupert must remember his Wife has gone. On the 21st in addition to the letter contained in this correspondence, he authorises Prince Rupert to press levies for 2,000 men to supply those now sent to his Majesty at Evesham. On the 22nd he recommends to Prince Rupert the relief of Lord Newcastle, and on the 23rd he confides the County of Gloucester to his care. **On the 24th the King addresses Rupert in a letter which** forms a part of this correspondence, and in it he again insists on a supply of 2,000 men. Apparently this reiterated command brought Rupert to Oxford; for we find him there on the following day, attending a Council of War, breathing his own brave spirit into its uncertain debates, proving to the King that he needed no more troops in Oxford and the West, and completing his arrangements for his expedition to the North.

Lord Grandison, whose letter to Prince Rupert immediately follows those of the King, was William Villiers, Viscount Grandison, son of Sir Edward Villiers, President of Munster, and Nephew of George Villiers, first Duke of Buckingham.

On the 10th August, 1642, twelve days before the Royal Standard was erected at Nottingham, Lords Carnarvon and Grandison received Commissions from the King to raise regiments of horse for the service of the Crown. Lord Lindsay had previously been made Lieutenant General of the Army, and Sir Jacob Asteley Serjeant Major General.

It was a time of anxiety and foreboding. Gathered round the person of their Sovereign were some of his wisest Councillors and some of his ablest Captains, but their was no unanimity in their advice, and no enthusiasm for their cause. They strove as best they might to bear the semblance of a Court, but the gloomy walls of a dismantled castle chilled their hopes, and frowned into failure every effort at the maintenance of ill timed state. A chapter of the Garter was held and the name of Rupert was blazoned on its knightly roll, but the formalities were irregular, the ceremonial was shorn of its customary splendour, and twenty years elapsed ere the proceedings of that day were amended and confirmed.

The King's standard was erected, but neither regal magnificence, nor heraldic pomp adorned that boding pageant—a few drums beat, a few trumpets sent forth their melancholy wail, and then to a scanty band of Gentlemen, and to an armed force of less than a thousand men, the Royal Proclamation was read, and the King submitted his cause, his crown, and his life to the stern arbitrament of war.

"Melancholy men," says Clarendon, "observed many ill presages about that time." The Royal cause indeed seemed hopeless ere the struggle was begun. The King had failed to seize on Hull; he had been ignominiously set at nought before the walls of Coventry; and now almost ere the strain of his trumpet had died away upon the air, came tidings that Portsmouth was delivered over to the Parliament by Goring, in whom he had fatally reposed his trust.

It was not, however, the danger of his cause that damped the spirits of the Noblemen and Gentry around him—some of these might say with Sir Edward Verney, the bearer of that ill omened standard, " For my part I do not like the quarrel, and do heartily wish the King would yield and consent to what they desire; so that my conscience is only concerned in honour and in gratitude to follow my master. I have eaten his bread, and served him thirty years, and will not do so base a thing as to forsake him, and choose rather to lose my life (which I am sure I shall do) to preserve and defend those things, which are against my conscience to preserve and defend."

Writing from Shrewsbury, on 21st Sept. following, the Earl of Sunderland thus expresses himself in a letter to his wife, "How much I am unsatisfied with the proceedings here, I have at large expressed in several letters; neither is there wanting daily handsome occasion to retire, were it not for gaining honour; for let occasion be never so handsome (unless a man were resolved to fight on the Parliament side, which for my part I had rather be hanged) it will be said, without doubt, that a man is afraid to fight. If there could be an expedient found to salve the punctilio of honour, I would not continue here an hour. The discontent that I and other honest men receive daily, is beyond expression."

Not among the Cavaliers alone was the approach of civil war regarded with reluctance and dismay. On a motion in Parliament in July, 1642, Whitelock, the historian, thus spoke—

"I look upon another beginning of our civil war, God blessed us with a long and flourishing peace, and we turned his grace into wantoness, and peace would not satisfy us without luxury, nor our plenty without debauchery; instead of sobriety and thankfulness for our mercies, we provoked the giver of them by our sins and wickedness to punish us (as we may fear) by a civil war, to make us executioners of divine vengeance upon ourselves."

"It is strange to note how we have insensibly slid into the beginning of a civil war, by one unexpected accident after another, as waves of the sea, which have brought us thus far; and we scarce know how, but from paper combats, by declarations, remonstrances, protestations, votes, messages, answers, and replies; we are now come to the question of raising forces, and naming a General, and officers of an army.

"We must surrender up our laws, liberties, properties, and lives into the hands of insolent Mercenaries, whose rage and violence will command us, and all we have, and reason, honour, and justice will leave our land; the ignoble will rule the noble, and baseness will be preferred before virtue, profaneness before piety."

"Of a potent people we shall make ourselves weak, and be the instruments of our own ruin, *perditio tua exte*, will be said to us; we shall burn our own houses, lay waste our own fields, pillage our own goods, open our own veins, and eat out our own bowels."

"You will hear other sounds, besides those of drums and trumpets, the clattering of armour, the roaring of guns, the groans of wounded and dying men, the shrieks of dishonoured women, the cries of widows and orphans, and all on your account which makes it the more to be lamented."

"Pardon, Sir, the remark of my expression on this argument, it is to prevent a flame which I see kindled in the midst of us that may consume us to ashes. The sum of the progress of civil war is the rage of fire and sword, and (which is worse) of brutish men."

There is more in the same strain from men who took prominent positions on either side; but the time for reflection, for expostulation, and for argument had passed, the hour of action had arrived, and Cavalier and Roundhead alike discarded all qualms as to the abstract justice of their cause, when engaged in struggle for victory and fame.

Soon after the raising of his standard, Charles left Nottingham and marched for Shrewsbury. He halted at Wellington, to enable his forces to assemble, and there, beneath the shadow of the Wrekin, addressed them as a soldier and their King. "I cannot," he said, "suspect your courage and your resolution; your conscience and your loyalty have brought you hither, to fight for your religion, your King, and the laws of the land * * * that you may see what use I mean to make of your valour, if it please God to bless it with success, I have thought fit to publish my resolution to you in a protestation; which when you have heard me make, you will believe you cannot fight in a better quarrel; in which I promise to live and die with you."

And then, in that stately language of which he was so great a master, he vowed to defend the Established Church, to govern by the laws, and protect the liberty of his subjects. He pledged himself, if it pleased God to "preserve him from the rebellion, to maintain the privileges and freedom of Parliament and govern according to law," and he solemnly added, "In the mean while, if this time of war, and the great necessity and straits I am now driven to, beget any violation of those, I hope it will be imputed by God and man to the authors of this war, and not to me; who have so earnestly laboured for the preservation of the peace of this kingdom. When I willingly fail in these particulars, I will expect no aid or relief from any man, or protection from Heaven. But in this resolution I hope for the cheerful assistance of all good men, and am confident of God's blessing."

The possession of Shrewsbury was of great moment to the King. Almost surrounded by the Severn which protected it on every side but one, it was an impregnable position so long as it was defended with resolution and skill. Occupied by an adequate force, it commanded a great reach of country, and formed one of the fortresses by which the line of the Severn was most easily guarded. It was among the most important in a series of cities which in former times had been regarded as barriers against the Welsh, and which in the days of which we are writing not only blocked the gates of warlike Wales against the enemy, but formed provincial capitals which were centres of government, of influence, and of thought. Originally the King, uncertain of the feelings of the inhabitants, hesitated whether to occupy that town or Chester, but on reaching Derby he had received such information as led him to select the former, and he never had reason to regret his decision. "A more general and passionate expression of affection cannot be imagined, than he received from the people of those counties of Derby, Stafford, and Shropshire as he passed; or a better reception than he found at Shrewsbury; into which town he entered on Tuesday, the 20th of September."

Shortly after the King's arrival, Lord Grandison was sent to the little town of Nantwich, in Cheshire, which the inhabitants had begun to fortify, and where the disaffected were drawing to a head. He acquitted himself with dexterity and skill, entering the town, taking the oaths of the inhabitants for their future obedience, destroying the half formed fortifications, and conveying all the arms and ammunition he could discover to Shrewsbury,

A few days after the capture of Marlborough, Lord Grandison, with his regiment, was taken prisoner, but shortly afterwards escaped to Oxford where the King then was resident, and resumed his place in the field.

At the assault on Bristol, in July, 1643, Lord Grandison, as Colonel General of the Foot, led the division of Prince Rupert in their attempt to storm the town. The attack was unsuccessful and Lord Grandison was slain. Clarendon writing of him says, "He was a young man of so virtuous a habit of mind, that no temptation or provocation could corrupt him; so great a lover of justice and integrity, that no example, necessity, or even the barbarity of this war, could make him swerve from the most precise rules of it; and of that rare piety and devotion, that the court or camp could not shew a more faultless person, or to whose example young men might more reasonably confirm."

The letter [No. 12] of Lord Derby was probably written during the march of Prince Rupert to the relief of York.

When the civil war broke out the Stanley influence was regarded as all prevailing in Lancashire and the adjacent districts. Lord Derby armed three regiments of foot and three of horse for the King, and in every action proved himself to be a gallant gentleman as well as a loyal subject. His strength had, however, been miscalculated; he did not command the love of his inferiors; he should have possessed the influence which great estates and long descent wield, when their owner is a man of honoured character and settled purpose, yet in *his* hands they served to make him an embarassing supplicant rather than an efficient supporter of the Crown. His letters for the most part are appeals for aid—he points out how much can be effected by others, he asks for arms, and he insists on the importance of the King's retaining his hold over Lancashire, while he apparently forgets that it was his own province to master that County, and vanquish the men who were there in arms for the Parliament He seems to have possessed no genius for war. Unenterprising, wanting in sympathy with those about him, without imagination or resource, his power was miserably wasted, and his plans were uniformly abortive.

In truth Lord Derby was a great noble but not a great man. We turn to another side of his character and find it in every way worthy of the race from which he sprung. His loyalty never wavered, his courage never quailed. He accompanied Rupert when the Prince raised the siege of Lathom house, and took Bolton by assault—in that action Lord Derby was the first man to take a colour from the enemy; at Marston he three times rallied his men and led them to the charge, and after that defeat he took refuge in the Isle of Man which he held for the Crown, and refused to surrender to the Parliament.

In July, 1649, Ireton made great offers to Lord Derby if he would surrender the Island and was answered in these words :—" I scorn your proffers, I disdain your favour ; I abhor your treason * * take this for your final answer, and forbear any further solicitations ; for, if you trouble me with any more messages of this nature, I will burn the paper, and hang up the messenger."

The siege of Lathom House is one of the most

picturesque incidents of the war. It was a castellated building of great strength, standing in a spongy basin, and was so much lower than the surrounding land that artillery could with difficulty be brought to bear upon it. It was defended by ten towers and surrounded by a deep moat. Into this stronghold, during the absence of her husband in the Isle of Man, the Countess of Derby threw herself, with a garrison of 300 men, and a few small pieces of ordnance. Shortly after his victory at Nantwich Sir Thomas Fairfax received peremptory orders from the Parliament to undertake the siege of Lathom, and accordingly on 28th February, 1644, he summoned Lady Derby to surrender, in a letter which was courteous as well as firm. She replied and by many ingenious devices contrived to delay the Parliamentary General, while she was completing her arrangements for the coming siege; when they were sufficiently formed she broke off all negociations, declaring that "though a woman and a stranger, divorced from her friends, and robbed of her estate, she was ready to receive their utmost violence, trusting in God for protection and deliverance."

In the meanwhile, Sir Thomas Fairfax was summoned to a nobler service than besieging a lonely lady in her Manor House; his Cousin, Sir William Fairfax, succeeded in command, but he too left on 24th March, and thenceforth the siege was left in charge of one Colonel Rigby.

Colonel Rigby was a Member of Parliament for Wigan. "He was a lawyer, and a bad one" says a contemporary, and he seems to have been quite as unsuccessful as a soldier as he had previously been in the law.

His first act was again to summon the Countess and her reply shews her estimate of him and his courtesy. When she received his letter she tore it up and exclaimed that the proper reward for Rigby would be to hang him at her gate. "Tell that insolent rebel," she continued, "he shall neither have person, goods, nor house; when our strength and provisions are spent, we shall find a fire more merciful than Rigby; and then, if the providence of God prevent it not, my goods and house shall burn in his sight; and myself, children, and soldiers, rather than fall into his hands, will seal our religion and loyalty in the same flame."

Next morning, at four o'clock, the soldiers sallied out upon the enemy. "There was one mortar piece which had raked them piteously and which they feared more than all the enemy's guns * * * the first thing they did was to make for the trench where this mortar piece lay guarded by fifty soldiers. After a quarter of an hour's fighting, they won the sconce, gained the rampart, levelled the ditch, and drawing up the iron monster by ropes dragged it into the house. The historian of the siege says, "Now neither ditches, nor ought else troubled our soldiers; their grand terror, the mortar piece, which had frightened them from their meat and sleep, lying like a dead lion, quietly among them; every one had his eye and foot upon it, shouting and rejoicing as merrily as they used to do with their ale and bagpipes. Indeed, every one had this estimation of the service, that the main work had been done, and what was yet behind was a mere pastime."*

The unhappy lawyer, on 1st May, wrote a piteous

---

* Momorials of the Civil War, Vol. 1, p. 90.

letter to the unsympathising deputy lieutenants of Lancashire—he had been compelled, he said, to borrow great and considerable sums of money both upon his word and bond for the public use. "We have had many nights together alarms, and beaten them into the house six and seven times in the night, and by these alarms and great numbers in the house, and by our losses, my soldiers have been inforced some to watch and stand upon the guard in the trenches for two nights together, and others two nights in four, in both which kind my son hath performed his duties as the meanest captain; and for myself I almost languish under the burden, having toiled above my strength." He concluded a long appeal by plainly intimating if they did not assist him that he should abandon the enterprise. Receiving no aid, on 27th May, he threw himself with his soldiers into Bolton.

The following day Rupert and Derby attacked the town, and after a fierce contest carried it; the Roundheads hung a royal trooper early in the day, and his death was sternly and bitterly revenged. Sixteen hundred of the garrison paid the penalty, and a few hours later twenty-two of the rebel colours which had waved in menace before Lathom House, were presented to the Countess to grace the stronghold she had so loyally and well maintained.

At a later date, when the great possessions of the House of Stanley were confiscated by the Parliament, the Isle of Man was granted to Sir Thomas Fairfax, "in public gratitude of his high deserts, and not as the issue of his own desires." He was a generous enemy, and declined to profit by the ill fortune of a noble race. He received the income of the Estates thus granted him,

D

but accounted to the Countess for every shilling he received; so that in after life she said she never received her rents with such regularity from her own agents. Fairfax never benefitted by the misfortunes of his Country, but declining to profit by the losses of others lived and died on the Estates bequeathed him by his predecessors.

Sir Jacob Astley (sometimes described as Ashley, and sometimes as Lord Astley or Ashley by the historians of the period) was the very type of an English Royalist.

Descended from an ancient and honored race, he was the second son of Isaac Astley, of Hill Morton and Melton Constable, and was born at the latter place in 1579.

When only 19 years of age he joined the forces which were sent by Queen Elizabeth to aid the people of Holland in their struggle against Philip of Spain. His distinguished gallantry led to his attaining at the hand of Maurice, Prince of Orange, the highest rank in his profession. In 1621 he associated himself with the gallant band of English gentlemen who fought nobly but in vain for the Elector Palatine; and ten years later he accepted a commission from the Duke of Hamilton, who fought under the banner of the great Protestant Champion, Gustavus of Sweden.

In 1641 he was summoned home to take a command in the expedition against the Scots, and when that breach was for the moment healed, he was given the Government of Plymouth, as a position of ease, honour, and emolument.

Already, however, the clouds were gathering which

were destined to break in the thunderstorm of civil war, and when the King's Standard was unfurled at Nottingham no truer or abler soldier ranged himself beneath it than the old soldier who, as a mere stripling, had 43 years before distinguished himself at the battle of Nieuport and the siege of Ostend.

In that noble series of characters which Clarendon has given us of his contemporaries we find Sir Jacob Astley thus described :—

"He was an honest, brave, plain man, and as fit for the office he exercised, of Major-General of the Foot, as Christendom yielded; very discerning and prompt in giving orders, as the occasion required, and most cheerful and present in any action. In council, he used few, but very pertinent words; and was not at all pleased with the long speeches usually made there, and which rather confounded than informed his understanding; so that he rather collected the ends of the debates, and what he was himself to do, than enlarged them by his own discourses; though he forbore not to deliver his own mind."

"He was purely a soldier and of a most loyal heart," writes another historian, and every trace of his career confirms these estimates of his character and conduct.

At the battle of Edgehill Sir Jacob Astley had the command of one of the divisions of Infantry, and did good service on that day of chequered fortunes and baffled hopes.

The hostile armies were in sight of each other, and the King addressed his own. "I have written and declared," said he, "that I intended always to maintain and defend the Protestant religion, the rights and privileges of Parliament, and the liberty of the subject, and now I must prove my words by the convincing argument of the sword. Let Heaven show its power by this day's victory to declare me just; and as a lawful, so a loving King to my subjects. The best encouragement I can give you is this: that come life or death, your King will bear you company, and ever keep this field, this place, and this day's service in his grateful remembrance."

And then, before the battle joined, the simple prayer of Astley rose fervently to Heaven, as the veteran said aloud, "Oh, Lord! Thou knowest how busy I must be this day; if I forget Thee, do not Thou forget me;" —and with that rose up, crying out, "March on, boys."

It has indeed been too much the custom to imagine that there were some broad, coarse lines of character and conduct which infallibly distinguished the Roundhead from the Cavalier. We can find none such; —the former counted among their number many a canting hypocrite, the latter included in their ranks many a godless and licentious knave,—thus it will ever be with the extremes of opposing parties,—and it is the worst or the weakest men who belong to them who generally exaggerate their own expressed opinions in the hope of inducing others to believe in their sincerity. To judge, however, that the quaint language and Scriptural phrases and images which the Roundheads employed were necessarily an evidence of hypocrisy would be a very transparent error. There was but little reading in those days among the masses, but the Bible was intensely studied; had any general literature or any historical knowledge been widely spread among them, it is probable their vocabulary would have been extended, and their views have been less founded on inspired history. As it was, the Bible was to them the sole standard of right and wrong, and the only historical parallels to which they could appeal were contained in it. The result was the exaggerated language which the Nonconformists employed, and which sounds so strange to us. That it was frequently used for evil ends, we doubt not; but in itself it was the natural result of the strained religious feeling and imperfect education of the period. If it be necessary further to support this view of the case, we would refer the reader to the common conversation of the Dissenters of the present day, and indeed to many of the Church-goers, in East Sussex; he will find there very similar causes have produced kindred effects, and that the same exclusive study of the Bible has induced a tone of thought and language which is in many respects curiously analogous to that which it effected in the 17th century.

The period was a deeply religious era, and there is no reason for attributing to the supporters of the Parliament any monopoly of serious and conscientious thought. No doubt, as time went on, and as feelings became embittered, each party strove to create or detect differences which might distinguish it from the other, and then the Sectaries became more and more self-righteous in their tone, and the followers of the King made it a matter of pride to scoff at their hypocrisy and cant, until the most violent among the former party might have graced a modern revival meeting, and the latter might have rivalled the frequenters of a betting booth.

This was, however, the gradual result of civil war

—of all strife the one most calculated to embitter the feelings and debase the actions of those who engage in it. The high-minded chivalry which marked Hopton, Grenville, Falkland, Astley, and many another noble gentleman who fought for the King, was equalled though it could not be surpassed by Essex, Fairfax, Denbigh, and Manchester, who strove for the Parliament. On both sides was the same great courtesy; on both the same stern resolution to do their duty; on both the same firm reliance on the justice of their cause; and the same solemn conviction that God would hold the balance and decide in favour of righteousness and truth. When, therefore, Sir Jacob Astley uttered his prayer on the field of Edgehill, we give him credit for unfeigned religious faith, and hold the act to be consistent not simply with his past life but with the spirit and convictions of the men among whom he had cast his lot.

The annals of the civil war are full of records of Astley: he was present in most of the more important battles, and his efforts to restrain the excesses of the Royalists, to secure supplies for and to attend to the comforts of his own soldiers, and to carry on the strife with humanity as well as with effect, are evidenced in numerous letters which are yet preserved. We will only pause to give a single extract from his letters.

Writing to Rupert on the 11th January, 1644-5, he expresses himself thus quaintly :—" Affter manie scolisietations by letteres and mesendgeres sent for better paiement of this garison, and to be provided with men, armes, and amonition for ye good orderinge and defence of this place, I have reseeived no comfort at all. So y^t in littell time our extreamieties must thruste the souldieres eyther to disband or mutiny, or plunder, and then yᵉ fault thereof wil be laied to my charge. God send ye Kinge mor monnie to go throw with his great worck in hande, and me free from blame and imputation."

Astley was, at different times, made Governor of various Royal Garrisons, and after the defeat of Naseby he was appointed Lieutenant General of the Royal forces in the West and on the Welsh Marshes.

At Worcester, many months after Rupert had surrendered Bristol, he collected a force of 3,000 men, with which he determined to join the King at Oxford, but his letters were intercepted and Sir Wm. Brereton and Colonel Morgan met him with an overwhelming force at Stow in the Wold, where, says Whitelocke, "after a sore conflict on both sides, Sir Jacob Astley was totally routed, himself taken prisoner, and 1,500 more horse and men, all their carriages, arms, and baggage taken. Morgan's word was "God be our guide," Astley's word was 'Patrick and George." * * * Sir Jacob Astley, after he was prisoner, told some of the Parliament Officers, ' Now you have done your work, and may go play, unless you fall out among yourselves.'"

And so it was—for there was now no army in the field to battle for the Crown—the high spirit of the Cavaliers was broken; there was discord in their councils and indecision in their Court. Henceforth the banner of the King might float for a brief period over an isolated castle, or a remote town, but the struggle was virtually over, and the defeat of Astley was the immediate forerunner of the final overthrow. In a letter of 6th June, 1646, the King, writing to him, says "the greatest of my misfortunes is that I cannot reward so gallant and loyal a subject as I ought and would."

He had, indeed, created him Baron Astley of Reading, (a title selected from the circumstance that he was descended from Thomas Baron de Astley, who was slain at the battle of Evesham in the reign of Henry III.) but beyond that empty honour he had nothing to bestow; a fugitive in his own land, a wanderer among his own people, he was soon to become the captive of his enemies, and the victim of his most relentless foes.

Astley remained some months a prisoner, and then was amnestied by the Parliament. He never drew the sword again, but was gathered to his fathers at a ripe old age, leaving behind him a name honoured by men of both parties, and a reputation which calumny itself never ventured to asperse.

Henry Hastings, Lord Loughborough, was a man of a widely different stamp. A son of the Earl of Huntingdon, he had all the advantages which rank and wealth conferred in those days on a great family. He enjoyed some popularity in his own neighbourhood, and among his own retainers, and his character was fertile in resources, enterprising, and undaunted.

He appears to have combined in a singular degree loyalty to the King with regard for his own interests; and the feud between the houses of Huntingdon and Stamford was carried on by him very effectually when he took up arms for the Crown. He fortified his father's house at Ashby de la Zouche, and in a short time raised a force sufficient to enable him to hold in check Lord Grey, the eldest son of the Earl of Stamford—the " King's service," says Clarendon, "being the more advanced there, by the notable animosities between the two families of Huntingdon and Stamford, between whom the County was divided passionately enough, without any other quarrel."

Clarendon notices his acts on three or four occasions; but Hastings does not figure in the stately portrait gallery the great historian has limned. We must gather our estimate of him from his acts, from the appreciation of his contemporaries, and from the letters which, written hastily and on the impulse of the moment, tell much of his disposition, his temper, and his aims.

The silence of Clarendon is unfortunate. A man in the position of Hastings, and taking an energetic part in the war, was the natural object of more than a passing comment. Yet beyond admitting his activity, and the local importance of his adhesion to the Royal cause, there is hardly a word about him in the History of the Rebellion.

Warburton, however, regards him as deserving all admiration, and thus expresses himself of his favourite hero. "Hastings was neither poor nor personally injured, it is true. He entered on the war with all the energy of a man who finds himself unexpectedly called upon to exert his peculiar talent; he was the model of a partizan leader; he kept the whole country round his father's stronghold at Ashby de la Zouche in awe. He possessed no scruples; he bore a blue banner blazoned with a furnace, and the candid motto, "*Qui ignis conflatoris*"—well suited to his fiery and destructive career. The Parliamentary Journals call him "that notable thief and robber."

We confess very reluctantly to have come to the conclusion that the Parliamentary was the more correct estimate of Hastings; and, although we find in Warburton and elsewhere evidences of his audacity and zeal, he appears to have deserved the opprobrium he earned and failed to redeem his character by any striking deed of successful daring.

One of the acts of this determined partizan leader was to enter Leicester on 22nd June, 1642, "with banners displayed and matches burning, and to read the King's Commission of Array." The Sheriff immediately read the Parliamentary decree against this Commission, and two messengers from the Parliament endeavoured, though without success, to capture Hastings. The scene is thus described by the messengers:—"Then the Cavaliers and the rest of the soldiers joining with the rude multitude, and about 24 parsons in canonicals, well-horsed, rode all towards the town with loud exclamations, 'A King! a King!' and others, 'For a King! for a King!' in a strange and unheard of manner, Captain Worsley giving the word of command to the soldiers,— 'Make ready, make ready; which, as they were proceeding to do, a sudden and extraordinary abundance of rain hindered the soldiers from firing * * * Then they followed Master Sheriff Chambers and Stanforth, crying out, 'At the cap! at the cap!' which was at that time on Chambers' head, and Master Hastings gave fire at Chambers with one of his petronels, but the same did not discharge."

Whitelocke's Memorials take the form of a diary, chronicling each day the events which were known in London; and in this work Hastings is constantly mentioned, *e. g.*—The last entry for February, 1643-4, is, " Sir John Gell routed a party of the King's horse under Colonel Hastings, took 120 horse, many prisoners and their arms." Ten days later Whitelocke records that "the Clergy and others being summoned to Leicester to take the covenant, and very many of them coming in, Colonel Hastings with 400 of the King's horse roamed about the country, and took about 100 prisoners of those that were going to take the covenant, and drove the rest home again. Upon this, about 200 horse were sent from Leicester, who unexpectedly fell into the quarters of Hastings, rescued all the prisoners, dispersed his troops, took 50 of them prisoners, and 140 horse and arms." According to the same historion an unusual misadventure befel him in the following October. " A party of Colonel Hastings his men came into Lougborough on the Lord's day, rode into church in sermon time, and would have taken the preacher away out of the pulpit, but the women rescued him, and proved then more valiant than their husbands, or Hastings his men."

It would be easy to multiply instances; but these which we have selected will suffice—they tell of a man whose energy was unrestrained by prudence, and whose enterprises were seldom illuminated by success.

Within three days after the defeat at Naseby, Hastings surrendered Leicester to Fairfax, an act which apparently displeased the King, for Whitelocke states on the following 13th August that " at Lichfield the King confined Colonel Hastings for delivering up of Leicester."

Lichfield had been captured by Rupert in April, 1643, after a gallant defence, and Colonel Henry Bagot had been appointed Governor of the place. Between Bagot and Hastings a fierce feud sprung up which was remembered with acrimonious resentment by the latter even after Bagot had met a soldier's death in the service of the Crown. On 25th July, 1645, writing from Lichfield to Rupert on the subject of an appointment, which we presume was that of successor to Bagot, he says, " I beseech you, Sir, give me leave to tell you that Town Adjutant Shrimshaw was the chief assistant Colonel Bagot used in his opposition against me, and our minds both too high to acknowledge a superiority, his present expressions declaring an impossibility of our agreement, which must needs be destructive to the King's service." What the result of this letter was we cannot say, but it is evident that the feuds at Lichfield were unappeased, and at length that they needed the intervention of Sir Jacob Astley to compose them.

The subsequent career of Hastings is the subject of several notes in Whitelocke. On 23rd February, 1645-6, the articles for the surrender of Ashby de la Zouche were received by the Parliament, and it was agreed that the estate of Colonel Hastings should be discharged of sequestration. He was again in arms, however, in 1648, and assisted in the gallant and vain defence of Colchester. He was taken prisoner when that town was surrendered to Fairfax, and Whitelocke states was banished the kingdom by the Parliament. However, he was at a little later date a prisoner in Windsor Castle, and escaped from that place on the evening of 30th January, 1649, the memorable day on which Charles perished on the scaffold.

James Stewart, Duke of Lenox, Hereditary High

Steward and High Admiral of Scotland, was nearly related to Charles. He was born in 1612, and having completed his education by foreign travel, returned to England.

He was born to great possessions, and added to them by his marriage to the daughter of the Duke of Buckingham. He was appointed Privy Councillor immediately on his return to England, and was subsequently made Lord Steward, Warden of the Cinque Ports, and created Duke of Richmond.

He was a most devoted subject and servant of the Crown. He had at his command all that could make life conspicuous. Youth, wealth, an ample patrimony, and an ancient and honoured name—yet without hesitation he perilled everything, except the last, in defence of the King he reverenced and the benefactor he loved.

Charles was guilty of grave faults and many weaknesses, but at least he won the attachment of faithful friends, and when he was convinced of their fidelity could repay it with confidence and trust; in the Duke of Richmond he recognised a kinsman bound to him by the recollection of past favours, and sincerely loyal to his person and his cause. Others had motives of selfishness to gratify or ambition to serve: one man desired to command his armies, another to control his councils, and a third to earn his gifts; each of them had some personal end to gratify, some private pique to avenge, or some exalted position to maintain or seize. Richmond stood alone; his wealth was sufficient for his needs, his position satisfied his pride, and he had no motive of interest or cupidity to color his advocacy or biass his mind,

He is spoken of by Clarendon as being in 1639 the only councillor about the King who "had the least consideration for his honour," and in 1641 as "almost the only man of great quality and consideration who did not in the least degree stoop or make court" to the Malcontents, "but crossed them boldly in the house." In the troubled scenes which then occurred he became the mark of repeated attacks, for he was known to be incorruptible, and it was felt he must therefore be disgraced. "His great and haughty spirit," unbending honour, and uncompromising speech, never quailed before the power, the insolence, or the intellect of the factions to which he was opposed.

When war broke out he attached himself to the person of the King. He had a great though silent influence in the little Court at Oxford, and his advice, as far as we can trace it, was sound and wise. He seems to have endeavoured to allay the feuds that recklessly weakened the royal cause, and, so far as Rupert was concerned, his aim was evidently to soothe his haughty and impracticable spirit, and to explain away the slights which might otherwise have led to serious discord in the camp as well as in the Court.

Richmond preserved his consistency of character and conduct to the last. He faithfully served the King in various negociations for peace with the Parliament; when Charles was in prison he unsuccessfully sued to be allowed to share his captivity, and when the regicides had passed their sentence the Duke vainly asked to be allowed to see his master and accompany him to the scaffold. He was present on the dreary day when the royal corpse was committed to the earth amid the sighs and silent prayers of a few weeping mourners, and then he left England to follow the fortunes of his master's son, and die of a broken heart in an alien land.

The Commission held by Rupert, the power it vested in him, and the extent to which he was subject to control was constantly matter of debate. The tone of the letter (No. 14) of the Duke dated Oxford, 21 April, is eminently that of a peace maker. Plans were certainly discussed at the Council, of the nature of those to which the Prince objected, but the intention was "to propound only by way of question all things of moment," and not to give orders to him about them. If the truth was spoken somewhat plainly on some points, they were points which the Council was acquainted with, such "as settinge downe the King's condition here" to a greater extent than Rupert—and even that discussion was held in the presence of William Legge, the most trusted servant and truest friend of the Prince.

Letter No. 18 must have been written on 18th September, 1643, for it states "Last night my Lord Digby writt to your Highness by the King's orders on the receipt of yours from Stamford," and Lord Digby's letter is dated 17th September, 1643.*

It was written at a critical period. After Rupert had won Bristol the Royal army, flushed with victory and confident of success, had beleaguered Gloucester. That city, surrounded by a ditch and a mouldering wall, was supposed to be incapable of defence, and after it had fallen the Cavaliers anticipated an easy and triumphant march to London. The fortifications of Gloucester were

---

* See Warburton History. Rupert and the Cavaliers, p. 290, vol. 3, where it is printed at length.

indeed slight, but brave hearts and willing hands were within those ancient walls, and a stern spirit animated Colonel Massey who held it for the Parliament, and his garrison of 1,500 men. On 10th August, 1643, out of "his tender compassion for his City of Gloucester" the King summoned it to surrender, offering pardon to all its garrison and inhabitants if the summons were complied with, and threatening to reduce the place by force unless within two hours the required submission was made.†

"Within less than the time prescribed, says Clarendon, together with the trumpeter returned two citizens from the town, with lean, pale, sharp, and bad visages, indeed faces so strange and unusual, and in such a garb and posture, that at once made the most severe countenances merry, and the most cheerful heart sad, for it was impossible such Ambassadors could bring less than a defiance. The men, without any circumstances of duty or good manners, in a pert, shrill, undismayed accent, said, "they had brought an answer from the godly city of Gloucester to the King," —and this answer which was signed by the Mayor, the Governor, and the principal inhabitants of the Town was to the effect that they held the city "to and for the use of his Majesty and his royal posterity," "and would" obey the commands of his Majesty, signified by both Houses of Parliament, and "were" resolved by God's help to keep the city accordingly.

The Letter from Lord Percy to the King (No. 35) gives an interesting detail of the progress of the siege, and the report of the Engineers upon the possibility of taking the city by storm.

---

† The account of the siege of Gloucester in May's History of the Parliament confirms that of Clarendon.

Meanwhile, there was anxiety and stern concentration of purpose among the energetic men who governed the decisions of the Parliament. Bristol had fallen, Gloucester was in peril, the House of Lords was clamouring for an accommodation with the King—but every pulpit rang with denunciations of peace; the walls of London were covered with inflammatory placards, and printed papers scattered through the streets summoned the people to rise as one man and support their chosen leaders. It was Sunday, yet on that day of rest the Common Council was assembled, and a petition to the Commons adopted "for the vigorous prosecution of the war, and declining all thoughts of accommodation."

The siege of Gloucester proceeded slowly, and before that city the army of the King revelled and wasted away. Irritated at the resistance they had encountered, the soldiery abandoned themselves to license and excess; thousands of sheep were wantonly destroyed; countrymen were imprisoned without warrant and held to ransom; and every species of severity was practised on the inhabitants of the district.

Animated by religious fanaticism and zeal for what they deemed to be the interests of their country, Massey and his gallant force defended themselves with energy and success; they burned the suburbs which might have sheltered the besieging army, they sallied out night after night upon their enemy, spiking cannon and killing the workmen in the trenches, while in all their labours, in all their dangers, the citizens took part with the soldiers, the women with their husbands, the children with their mothers.*

---

*Guizot's English Revolution, p. 201, edit. 1846.

Meanwhile the haughty Essex placed himself at the head of the army of relief. Brave, undemonstrative, and coldly determined to do his duty, he asked no sympathy from his employers, but won from them their confidence and trust. His letters are models of business communications; they dwell on every point that demands attention, they enumerate the requirements of the army and its chief; and state briefly, but with accuracy, the events which have occurred and the designs which are in progress. He never magnifies his own successes, never incumbers his letters with stilted professions of his zeal for "The Cause," and makes no canting allusion to interpositions from Heaven in favour of Parliament and the leaders they trusted to command their armies. In short, an aristocrat at heart and a patriot from principle, he was too honest to conceal his sentiments, and too proud to pander to the follies and vices of his Employers.

On 24th August Essex mustered his army on Hounslow Heath; his forces numbered about 15,000, but in great part they were men hastily levied, imperfectly drilled, and unused to the toils and perils of war. With this army of conscripts he marched for Gloucester.*

Through a country devastated by friend and foe; over wide plains where the cavalry of the enemy might have cut off his supplies and possibly destroyed his army; and in face of a victorious enemy and their exasperated

---

* The date given by Warburton in Rupert and the Cavaliers is 24th August, vol. 2, p. 285.

In the lives of the Devereux, Earls of Essex vol. 2, p. 378, the mustering at Hounslow is dated 15th Aug., and the March from Aynhoe 2nd Sept. In Carlyle's Cromwell the date of the march is given 26th Aug., vol. 1, p. 145, edit. 1873. Whitelocke p. 72, edit. 1732, states Essex marched from Aylesbury on 29th March, and Clarendon, without giving the precise date, apparently confirms Whitelocke.

King, Essex marched and fought his way. On the evening of September 5th his signal fires blazed from the heights of the Cotswold hills, and the boom of his cannon announced to the beleaguered city that succour was at hand.

The royal army burned their huts that night, and on the 8th Essex entered Gloucester. A few days longer delay would have been fatal, for the defenders were well nigh worn out, their provisions were exhausted, and their store of gunpowder was reduced to the last barrel. The city might probably have been taken by storm when Lord Percy's letter was written, but the King shrank from the bloodshed such a step would have involved, and wasted his men and his resources on an ineffectual blockade. Rupert, who with characteristic impetuosity, had urged an assault, declined to be responsible for a course he disapproved, and acted during the siege only as Commander of the Horse.

A determined attack on the Parliamentary forces when they were toiling across the open country on their way to Gloucester would probably have been successful; the King and his advisers, however, miscalculated the purposes and power of their enemy. Charles had gravely replied to the deputies from Gloucester, "If you expect help you are deceived; Waller is extinct, and Essex cannot come;" and even when it was known that the latter General was on the march, he supposed it was a mere demonstration, and that its only purpose was to threaten Oxford, and induce him to march in its defence and thus to raise the siege. When at length the King realized the fact that Essex seriously purposed to relieve the city, he still was unconscious of the imminence of the danger, for on 5th September, the very day on which Essex reached the hills above Prestbury, Charles in a letter dated "Matson, 5th September, 10 morn," thus wrote to Prince Rupert* "The General is of opinion that we shall do little good upon this town, for they begin to countermine us, which will make it a work of time; wherefore he is of opinion, to which I fully concur, that we should endeavour to fight with Essex as soon as may be, after we have gotten our forces together, which I hope will be to-morrow, those from Bristol being already come; the greatest care will be to meet with him before he can reach the hedges; now if this be your opinion, as it is ours, which I desire to know with all speed. I desire you to do all things in order to it that no time be lost."

Before this letter reached the Prince, Essex must have gained the enclosed country where the royal Cavalry could annoy him but little,—and Gloucester was saved.

Urged by the fatal importunity of Rupert, Charles resolved to give battle to the enemy and cut off his return to London. By means of forced marches which fatigued his troops, he intercepted Essex at Newbury, and fought a disastrous battle there. In vain did the impetuous Cavaliers charge time after time the dense masses of the city train bands; valour, chivalry and long descent could not give them the victory over the stubborn courage of those massed pikemen; and every charge saw their numbers lessen, and the steady courage of their foe confirmed.

At last night fell and the King withdrew his forces

---

* Rupert and the Cavaliers, v, 2, p. 286.

into the neighbouring Town. Then, indeed, he had time to think upon his losses, though he had not the opportunity to count his dead. Falkland was among the slain, and found that peace at length for which his weary spirit had vainly sought on earth; Sunderland had satisfied "the punctilio of honour," and the "great parts, the virtue," and the varied powers of Carnarvon slept in his early grave.

The King is stated to have lost 2,000 men upon that fatal day, and although both parties claimed it as a victory, Essex remained in possession of the field, and gave orders for the burial of the dead. Sullenly the royal army withdrew, leaving the road open to their enemies, and in a few days time Essex entered London in triumph.

The letter (No. 19) of the Duke of Richmond of the 25th March, 1644, relates to the relief of Newark, a deed which was most worthy of panegyric, but which has already been referred to. We have already stated that Rupert largely increased his army in Shropshire and the Western Counties. It must not, however, be supposed that men of less energy and singleness of purpose would have been equally successful. Before his arrival the Royalist leaders uttered nothing but complaints; every thing was required, nothing was to hand. Disputes among themselves seem to have occupied whatever time their enemy allowed them to enjoy, and the only sentiment they shared in common was an anxious desire for the arrival of the Prince, and the consequent shifting of responsibility from their shoulders to his.

On 25th January the Prince wrote to Sir Francis

Ottley, Governor of Shrewsbury, announcing that the King had intrusted to his care his army in Shropshire and the Counties adjacent, together with his interest there. He referred to some plot for the betrayal of the town to the enemy, and then added, "but I do not hear they (the conspirators) are brought to justice by any proceeding against them, so that the punishment may be to some—the example and terror to all," and he intimates that the Town will be his head quarters and that he requires certain alterations made in the Castle to fit it for the reception of stores, together with the erection of huts as lodgings for the garrison. On the receipt of this letter the Governor prevailed upon the inhabitants to assess themselves at £1,000 for the service of the King. Sir John Mennes, however, a few days later, states that "his Highness must be seen here, and I think felt too, before this hard hearted people will believe he is coming." The same luckless gentleman remarks in another letter "money is a thing not spoken of, neither do I perceive your Highness' last letter prevailed at all with them * * I must crave pardon if I quit the place for I have not wherewithal to subsist any longer, having received but £22 now in eleven months, and lived upon my own without free quarters for horse or man. The fortune I have is all in the rebells' hands, or in such tenants as have forgot to pay."

The truth was that all parties, save those who hoped to gain personally by it, were very weary of the war. The longer it continued the smaller seemed the chances of eventual peace. Armies traversed the country, assailed and battered down castles, burned towns and villages, and laid waste woods and corn fields. There was the excitement of the conflict for those engaged in it, fierce exultation for the victor, and possibly hope for the vanquished, but what had the peaceful citizen to gain by all this confusion and blood? What cared the yeoman whose farm steading was committed to the flames for the doubtful claims of Royalist or Parliamentary combatant? What knew the husbandman of precedent or privilege, of the rights of the people, or the prerogative of the Crown?

The first burst of enthusiasm on either side was over, and the prosaic realities of war came home to an impoverished and heartsick people. It is well for men who regard war as a pageant and not as a reality, to write in glittering language of glancing banners and towering crests, to tell us that the trumpet call of Rupert was worth a thousand men, and to compare the freebooters, who ranged themselves beneath his flag, with the mythical combatants of a more chivalrous era. How did these facts present themselves to the men who without taking part in, were sufferers by the war? The Parliament had great pecuniary advantages over the King, yet the pay of the soldiers was constantly in arrear, and "outrages, which no authority under such circumstances could restrain, continued to spread dismay through the country." The condition of the army of the Crown may be gathered from a thousand sources, everywhere there is the same complaint, "our soldiers' pay is in arrear, our own means are exhausted, without money we cannot continue the struggle unless indeed we make the war support itself.' Eloquent is the accidental testimony of the actors in this great tragedy, and such expressions as those of Lord Grandison, "these are the reasons that keep me a day longer in this burnt and plundered quarter," penned as they were with a far different purpose, show us how much the country suffered at the hands of the combatants.

The time had arrived when Rupert was to measure himself against the armies of the North. In Lancashire, Lathom House was besieged by the enemy, and its fall would have injured the cause of Charles far more than its real importance merited, for it would have been construed into an evidence of incapacity on the part of the King to protect one of the most important and loyal families in the land Rupert, as we have already seen, accomplished this design, and thus far preserved his character for valour and success. He now had an enemy to face of another kind from Mr. Rigby of Preston, and his routed forces. Sir Thomas Fairfax was a soldier, a patriot, and a gentleman, he was as brave as Rupert, without his rashness; as honest as Hampden, and as generous as Newcastle. A stern disciplinarian, he shrunk from no peril or hardship to which his soldiers were exposed, and obtained over them the mastery which indomitable courage, generosity, and kindly feeling ever win from men who have the heart to recognize and the discernment to honour them. Fairfax was no Statesman, and at Westminster others won the prizes in ambitions fevered race, he did not covet them, and stood proudly aloof from every cabal. His cause was his country's good, his sword was ever at her service, and through evil report and good report he followed the dictates of his honour and his conscience. Lord Leven commanded the Scotch and the Earl of Manchester (under whom served Cromwell) commanded an independent army which had recently taken Lincoln. The combined forces of the three Generals is estimated to have amounted to about 30,000 men, and they laid siege to York.

The Prince marched rapidly on York, united Goring's troops with his own, avoided the hostile armies, and entered the city without a battle. This success might well have contented him. The siege was raised, the enemy out-generalled, and if he had reinforced the garrison his army was free for other enterprises. The Marquis of Newcastle was a man of mark and valour; his second in command, General King Lord Eythin, was a soldier of approved reputation and skill. York might well have been left to their care, and Essex and Waller might have felt the weight of Rupert's sword. But no! ever impetuous, ever rash, ever anxious for battle the Prince would listen to no counsel, and be guided by no experience save his own. Within a very short time after the letter from Newcastle was received Prince Rupert met him in York, Newcastle urged him to be satisfied with the success he had achieved; "discord he said was working in the camp of the enemy; the Scots were on bad terms with the English, the Independents with the Presbyterians; Lieutenant General Cromwell with Major General Crawford; if he must fight let him at least wait for a reinforcement of 3,000 men which must shortly arrive." With scanty courtesy Rupert overruled the Marquis, alleging the King's command was that he should fight in any event, and, ordering the troops to march, he accompanied them to Marston Moor.

The letter on which the Prince relied was couched in the following terms:

"Ticknell, 14th June, 1644,

"Nepheu*

"First I must congratulate with you, for yor good successes, assuring you, that the things themselves

---

* Evelyn's Diary and Corresponence, vol. 4, p. 141.

are no more welcom to me, then that your are the meanes. I know the importance of supylying you with powder, for wh^ch I have taken all possible wayes, have sent both to Ireland and Bristoll. As from Oxford this bearer is well satisfyed that it is impossible to have at present, but if he tell you that I may spare them from hence, I leave you to judge, having but 36 left; but what I can get from Bristoll (of wch there is not much certainty it being threatned to be besieged) you shall have.

"But now I must give you the trew state of my affairs, wch if their condicion be such as enforces me to give you more peremptory comands then I would willingly doe, you must not take it ill. If York be lost, I shall esteeme my Crown little lesse, unless supported by your suddain march to mee, and a miraculous conquest in the south, before the effects of the northern power can be found here, but if York be relieved, and you beat the Rebels' armies of both kingdoms wch are before it; then, but otherwise not, I may possibly make a shift (upon the defensive) to spin out time, untill you come to assist me. Wherefore I comand and conjure you by the duety and affecion wch I know you beare me that (all new enterprises layd aside) you immediately march (according to yor first intention) with all your force to the reliefe of York; but if that be either lost, or have freed themselves from the besiegers, or that for want of powder you cannot undertake that work; that you immediately march with your whole strength to Worster, to assist me and my army, without w^ch, or yor having relieved York by beating the Scots, all the successes you can afterwards have most infallibly will be useless unto me. You may beleeve that nothing but an extreeme necessity could make me write thus unto you, wherefore, in this case, I can no wayes doubt of your punctuall compliance with.

"Your loving Uncle & most faithful frend,
"CHARLES R."

This letter was written by the King at perhaps the most critical moment of his military career. Secretly marching out of Oxford, which was then threatened with a siege, he made his way to Worcester, and appeared bent on reaching Shrewsbury. His sudden departure drew the Parliamentary armies after him, and for the moment saved Oxford. The movement commenced in flight, though afterwards it assumed the form of an offensive operation, and has been described as masterly and successful strategy on the part of the King. Exactly one week before the date of this letter the Duke of Richmond thus wrote from Worcester to the Prince, "We want money, men, conduct, diligence, provisions, time, and good counsel. Our hope rests chiefly in your good success." A letter written by Lord Digby on the 8th, after giving an account of the proceedings since the resolution to quit Oxford was adopted, and stating that the Royal forces consisted of 2,000 musketeers and 2,500 horse, besides the garrison of Evesham, and that that town had been abandoned to, and Tewkesbury occupied by, the enemy, proceeds—"When I shall have told your Highness this and that Essex comes upon us one way, Waller likely to go about us on the Welsh side of Gloucester, that Massey and the Lord Denbigh towards Kidderminster, both with considerable forces; and when to all this I shall add the uncertainty as yet of your Brother's succeeding before Lyme, and that Oxford is scarce victualled for a month, and, for ought we know, blocked up in a manner by the enemy's horse, your Highness will easily frame to yourself an image of our sad condition; all hopes of relief to which, depend upon your Highness' happy and timely success, which his Majesty is resolved to expect by defending this place with his foot, unless there shall be an opportunity given them of putting them into Bristol and joining them with Prince Maurice, and then remove with what horse and dragoons he can make, according as the event shall give him the opportunity of doing it with most safety."

A few days later Essex marched to Salisbury and thence to Lyme and Plymouth, while Waller, with insufficient numbers, was left to watch the King. Charles availed himself of the opportunity thus offered him, and on 29th June, at Cropredy Bridge, near Banbury, inflicted a defeat upon his enemy, and a few days later moved westward, intending to do battle with Essex who was besieging Exeter.

The letter of the King was couched in far more imperative terms than those he ordinarily employed. In the letters now published he says he is very much "pleased with a proposition, but will not conclude it without your advice." "I would not have you to judge by our foolish discourses here, but doe according to your owen judgement." "I offer for your consideration whether you will not rather bend towards Yorkshire to save my Lord Newcastle & to beat the Scots, then to reduce Lancashire." In this communication however, instead of consulting his Nephew, Charles excuses himself for giving him peremptory commands; he tells him if York falls his Crown will follow, and therefore commands and conjures Rupert to march to the relief of that city; it is clear, too, that he thinks the defeat of the Scotch army absolutely necessary for the preservation of the Town for the only chance he has of spinning out time depends on his Nephew relieving York and beating the rebel armies of both Kingdoms which were before it—and at the end of the letter he repeats the same idea, for he adds "if that York be lost or you cannot undertake that work, immediately march with your whole strength to Worcester to assist me and my army; without which, or your *having relieved York by beating the Scots*, all the success you can afterwards have must infallibly be useless to me." The language of the letter appears to countenance the construction Prince Rupert placed upon it, and the desperate condition of the King's affairs may to some extent justify the risk so fatally run—but every leader of an army is bound to use discretion even in obeying orders, and the battle of Marston as fought and lost evidenced neither the prudence of a man of the world, nor the skill and military qualities of a great general.

The day after the battle, Clarendon states that Prince Rupert and the Marquis sent messages to one another,* "the one that he was resolved, that morning, to march away with his horse, and as many foot as he had left; and the other, that he would, at that instant, repair to the sea side, and transport himself beyond the seas; both which they immediately performed." Lord Eythin accompanied the Marquis, upon which,† "they who were content to spare the Marquis poured out all the reproaches of infidelity, treason, and conjunction with his countrymen which, without doubt, was * * without the least foundation, or ground for any such reproach * * he had

---

* Clarendon, vol. 4, p. 512.
† Clarendon vol. 4, p. 521.

been prosecuted by some of his countrymen with the highest malice, from his very coming into the King's service, and the same malice pursued him after he had left the Kingdom, even to his death." It was evidently a report that the Prince had given countenance to these rumours that called forth Lord Eythin's remonstrance of 23rd of January, 1645 [No. 22.]

The letter of 28th March [No. 25] was written by Sir Samuel Tuke, a Colonel in the King's Service. General Porter, to whom it is addressed, commanded a regiment of the Marquis of Newcastle's foot at Marston, and at different times held offices of trust for the Crown. Differences arose between him and his superior officer, Lord Goring, and each of them impeached the loyalty and honour of the other. Porter did his best to justify Lord Goring's charges against him, by quitting his command in October 1645 and hastening up to London and making his peace with the Parliament. Goring, whose career was a long succession of curiously varied treacheries, deserted his post at the same time and retired to France; almost his last official act was to issue an order under which £200 was paid to Porter, a sum that worthy gentleman employed to defray the cost of his journey to London and his submission to the Parliament.

Sir Samuel Tuke was a faithful servant of the King. In 1648 he was one of the leaders of the Royalists in the insurrection which closed so tragically in Colchester. He died 25th January, 1670, and was a man of some consideration after the restoration. Pepys, in his diary under date 1st February, 1668-9, says, "at the change, I did at my booksellers shop accidentally fall into talk with Sir Samuel Tuke about trees and Mr.

Evelyn's garden, and I do find him, I think, a little conceited, but a man of very fine discourse as any I ever heard almost; which I was mighty glad of." He was a cousin of John Evelyn, in whose correspondence and diaries there are many references to him.

Daniell O'Neille, the writer of the letter numbered 26, was a gentleman of independent means, great daring, and a strong disposition for political intrigue. Before the war broke out he was no favorite with Charles, for he was of the number of those who hunted Strafford to his doom, but when the troubles began, and before a sword was drawn, he perilled liberty and life in the service of the King.

He was concerned in 1641 with Digby, Wilmot, Goring, and Ashburnham in "the army plot," the object of which was to support the King, uphold the Church, and overawe the Parliament. In a letter of Sir Edward Nicholas to the King, of 27th September, 1641, he states that O'Neille and Sir J. Berkeley had been the day before at Weybridge, "I was bould then," he adds, "to deliver my opinion to ye Queene, that I did beleeve if they continued in England they would be arrested," and two days later he mentions that they had been arrested on the 28th, "and ye committees would not bayle them, though they tendered it, alledging they had not power to doe it." In the margin of this letter the King wrote " I hope some day they may repent their severetie." On 19th November Nicholas again wrote on this subject, "The business against O'Neall is referred to a select comittee to be prepared ready for ye House against Monday next, and some think it will be hardly heard then, for albeit ye Comons have a very good minde to proceede roundly against him, yet (I heare) ye proofs are so broken, as they will not make a full and cleare evidence., the worst in all that business is, that it reflects on your Majestie, as if you had given some instruccions concerning ye stirring up ye army to petition ye Parliament. I hope it will appear that your Majestie's intencions were only to reteyne ye army in their duty and dependance on your Majestie."

The tone of the letter is a curious example of the want of confidence his adherents felt in Charles. It is clear that Nicholas was quite unaware of the nature of the letters referred to, and thought it perfectly possible that the King might have imprudently sanctioned the plot in which the Parliament pronounced it treason to participate.

O'Neille extricated himself from his embarassing position by escaping from the Tower in woman's clothes, and when a few months later the King raised his standard O'Neille returned to England and accepted a commission as Lieutenant Colonel of Horse under Rupert.

At different times during the war we find traces of him. In 1643 he accompanied the Earl of Antrim to Ireland and superintended the dispatch of 1,500 men to the Marquis Montrose, who with their aid set up his standard in Scotland, and won back half that nation to the King. At Marston he led Prince Rupert's regiment of foot, and in 1658 he accompanied the Marquis of Ormonde in disguise to London and remained there some time, holding meetings with the Royalists and sounding them as to the prospect of a successful rising against Cromwell. After the restoration the following entry in

Pepys' diary seems to imply that O'Neille was a person of some account. "July 3rd, 1662, dined with the officers of the Ordnance, where Sir W. Compton, Mr. O'Nealle, and other great persons were."

The surrender of Bristol by Prince Rupert is the subject of the finding of the Council of war, held at Newark, on 21st October, 1645.

On 14th June the battle of Naseby had been fought. Although the forces engaged in it were not so numerous as those which contended at Marston, the consequences of the defeat was far more momentous. Marston deprived the Marquis of Newcastle of the north of England. Naseby cost Charles his kingdom. The defeat was complete and crushing; every regiment lost its colors; the royal standard and those of the Palatine Princes were captured; nearly 6,000 men were slain or taken prisoners; 8,000 stand of arms, ammunition, stores, and above all the secret correspondence of the King fell into the hands of the enemies, while the King and Prince Rupert with difficulty fled to Hereford.

At length the time had arrived when brave men acknowledged that the struggle was hopeless. Even Rupert bowed his hitherto tameless spirit and vainly counselled peace. "If I were desired," he said in a letter to the Duke of Richmond dated 28th July, "to deliver my opinion what other wayes the King should take, this should be my opinion, which your Lordship may declare to the King. His Majesty hath now no way left to preserve his posterity, kingdom, and nobility, but by a treaty."

There were, it is true, a few evil councillors left

who still urged the King to continue his resistance; chief among these men was Lord Digby, but even he, while insisting upon his own views, thus describes the feeling of the Royalists. "These hopes, I am confident, the condition of our business itself will bear, would the humours of our own party bear them with patience. But, alas! my Lord, we must not expect it, there is such an universal weariness of the war, despair of a possibility for the King to recover, and so much of private interest grown from these upon everybody, that I protest to God I do not know four persons living besides myself and you that have not already given clear demonstration, that they will purchase their own, and, as they flatter themselves, the kingdom's quiet, at any price to the King—to the Church—to the faithfulest of his party; and to deal freely with you, I do not think it will be in the King's power to hinder himself from being forced to accept such conditions as the rebels will give him, and that the next news that you will hear, after we have been one month at Oxford, will be, that I and those few others, who may be thought by our counsels to fortify the King in firmness to his principles shall be forced or torn from him."

If, however, the King resolved to throw a last cast for empire he should at least have perservered in some decided and manly policy. Several courses were open to him; none were free from danger, few presented much prospect of ultimate success; a daring spirit, however, would have risked the evil they menaced, on the chance however remote, of winning the results they promised as the guerdon of success. Three distinct lines of action were open to Charles. In Devon and Cornwall Goring still commanded 7,000 or 8,000 men; the presence of the King would have kindled into enthusiasm the decaying loyalty of the West, he would have controlled the mad excesses of his profligate General, and composed the differences which threatened to disintegrate his armies. Such action was full of peril. The conquering forces of Fairfax, and the invincible ironsides of Cromwell would certainly have swept down upon the King and his last army—and slight would have been the chances of the Western levies when opposed to those veteran and unconquered battalions. Even now every post bore him tidings of some fresh disaster, and, from the fatal hour when his power was shattered at Naseby, each day that dawned seemed charged with messages of humiliation and loss. What then were his chances of success? The Scotch army was at Hereford, Goring had failed to save Bridgewater; and while the King pondered over a Western Campaign the defeat at Lamport stamped the impulse with a boding whisper of defeat. It was a desperate venture and Charles could not resolve to face it. The alternative which had its advocates and advantages was to rouse the loyal inhabitants of Wales; to gather an army in the mountains of Carmarthen and the fertile plains of Monmouth, and beneath the sheltering walls of Ragland to marshall them for a new campaign. The King determined to follow out this policy, and it was in truth well suited to his character and temperament. The great influence of the Marquis of Worcester and his son, impaired though it was by the religion they professed, had enormous weight in Monmouth and the surrounding counties. They had made sacrifices for the royal cause unparalleled even in the history of that period of generous self oblivion; they were the natural leaders of a people who were loyal as well as warlike; and amid the stately terraces and towers of Ragland, Charles could for a moment forget that he was a fugitive, and persuade himself that with another effort he could re-win his kingdom and his crown.

Charles was no coward; he proved his courage on occasions where danger beset him, and neither in battle nor in retreat did he ever disgrace himself or his royal lineage by shrinking, when they were forced upon him, from peril, anxiety, or risk. Nevertheless his mind was not cast in a heroic mould, and the course which promised present ease, and offered a fair prospect for the future, had far greater attractions for him than more daring and vigorous action. Thus the King accepted the hospitality of his great feudatory, and feasted, hunted, and held his court in Ragland. The noblemen and gentry of the counties round resorted to him there and pledged their faith to him anew, and promised to recruit the ranks which had been so grievously thinned by folly, improvidence, and war.

Such promises could have deceived no one who dispassionately appraised their worth. The counties from which this new army was to spring had already been drained of a large part of its youth and vigour; regiments had gone forth from thence to serve through arduous campaigns, only to be decimated at Marston, or destroyed at Naseby; and it was as unreasonable to expect a repetition of these efforts, as to look for the physical strength of youth in the enfeebled frame of the aged Marquis. The country in fact was worn out, and could not have redeemed the promises made for it to the King even if it had the will to do so, and his cause had been surrounded with the prestige of success.

INTRODUCTION.

Besides the exhaustion of the country another influence was working against the King, the influence of his most unfortunate temperament.

As though some malignant spirit had power over him, it was the hapless destiny of Charles to say nothing and do nothing without equivocation or mental reserve. He never committed himself with a whole heart to any policy but had always some unacknowledged plan to depend on if the plans he presented failed; while if they succeeded his alternative scheme was intended to modify their effect. No one possessed his whole confidence. At the moment of which we are now writing he had lost the sympathy of the Western army and the counties from which it was drawn, by the discovery that he was treating with the Confederate Catholics in Ireland for the despatch of a Catholic army to the coast of Devon; an army which men like Lord Hopton were expected to join, or to which they were possibly to cede their position as the army of the Crown.

Simultaneously with this mad and reckless insult to the protestant feeling of the country, Charles estranged the loyalty of the Welsh by a more open act of perverse folly. He received intelligence that Hereford must surrender to the Scotch army unless relieved within a month, and he therefore directed the Sheriffs of the adjoining counties to summon the *posse comitatus* in order by that means, with the assistance of the Cavalry who were with him, to raise the siege. A meeting was held at Cardiff and upwards of 4,000 attended. Before they consented to take up arms, they made representations of the injuries they had received from General Gerrard, and the exactions he laid upon them. The representations were true, and the King reluctantly substituted Lord Astley for the General. So far he did what was wise, but in the same breath he conferred a peerage upon Gerrard, thus irritating the very men from whom he was asking assistance, and alienating them from his cause at the moment their aid was vitally important to the success of his enterprise.

Having alienated both the districts whence he had hoped to recruit his armies, Charles turned his thoughts northward, and resolved to join Montrose.

The men that gallant adventurer had obtained from Lord Antrim had enabled him to do everything short of winning a kingdom. Few as were his troops in number, deficient in arms, and wanting in discipline, in his hands they were more effective than the dense battalions of the Covenanters. He routed Elcho who had 6,000 men under his command; defeated Burleigh; ravaged the country of Argyle and defeated him at Innerlochy; marched 60 miles without rest or food in face of an enemy whose overwhelming number rendered attack on him impossible; gained successive victories over Urrie and Baillie. and finally on 15th August defeated the whole of his enemy at the sanguinary battle of Kilsyth. At length Scotland was almost won; the nobles, who had hitherto feared to avow themselves, hastened to range themselves by his side; Edinburgh opened her gates and released the imprisoned Royalists; the King's Commission was proclaimed, and Montrose was recognized as Lieutenant Governor and Captain General of Scotland.

Montrose was in the full career of his victories

when the King, with such forces as he could collect, marched northward. Had he persevered in his design and pushed on w th resolution and despatch he would have joined Montrose a few days after the victory of Kilsyth, and, perhaps, his presence might have changed the issue of the war. Again, however, his fatal irresolution betrayed him. He was induced to waste time in Welbeck and Doncaster, and at the latter place tidings reached him that Leslie and the Scotch horse were only ten miles off. These horse were hurrying into Scotland to arrest the tide of Montrose's victories, and uphold the failing cause of the Covenant. Wearied with marching, and dispirited with the evil news which had summoned them from Hereford, the army of Leslie could ill have resisted had the King attacked them. Charles, however, made no inquiries; he assumed the Scotch were in pursuit of him, so he turned his horses head and fled to Oxford.

The King was in this, his city of refuge, when he learned that Fairfax was besieging Rupert in Bristol—"for which nobody" (says Clarendon) "underwent any trouble; for all men looked upon that place as well fortified, manned, and victualled; and the King even then received a very cheerful letter from Prince Rupert; in which, he undertook to defend it full four months. So that the siege being begun so late in the year as the beginning of September, there was reasonable hope that the army might be ruined, before the town taken."*

As early, indeed, as the 28th July Rupert had written to Colonel Legge, who was Governor of Chester, "We were never in better condition than now. All our officers

---

* Clarendon, vol. 5, p. 249.

and soldiers are paid and billeted in town," and it appears that until after the siege was formed he was confident of being able successfully to defend the city.* It was indeed a possession to be maintained at any risk; it was the most important port in the kingdom save London; it was the door through which the Continent could be reached, and communications be most easily held with Ireland, and through it had come most of the muskets, ammunition, and stores which had enabled the King to maintain the war.

We learn from a declaration published by Prince Rupert that his garrison consisted of 2,300, "but after the enemy approached, his Highness could never draw upon the line above 1,500, and it was impossible for his Highness to prevent them from getting over the works; and many of them were new levied Welsh, and inexperienced men." Some writers, however, represent the force under his command at about 4,000 men.†

The old city of Bristol stands between the Avon, which bounds it on the West, and the Frome on the East, in a species of peninsular formed by those two rivers. On the South, where the two rivers meet, was some waste ground called the marsh, while on the North a deep canal from the Avon to the Frome protected the city from attack; beyond the canal was the castle, surrounded by a broad moat and fortified by massive walls. The old city appears to have been surrounded by fortifications of no great strength.

When the war broke out, Colonel Fiennes, who held the city for the Parliament, erected an outer ring of

---

* Warburton's Prince Rupert, vol. 3, p. 151.
† Markham's Fairfax, 246 note.

fortifications; they consisted of a wall and moat and ten towers, besides redoubts. These forts and the castle mounted 110 guns, and the line to be defended was about four miles in length. Prince Rupert in his declaration alleged that his supply of ammunition was reduced to 136 barrels, which was insufficient for a siege of any duration; that the fortifications were for the most part only three feet high but never exceeded five feet; that the ditch was nowhere deeper than five feet or wider than seven feet; and that the highest portions of the forts were not more than twelve, nor the curtains more than ten feet high. Notwithstanding the conditions of the fortifications the judgment of the Colonels of Posts was, "that notwithstanding the works and line were very defective, the circuit large, our numbers few, yet if we could repel one general storm, the enemy would be discouraged from attempting the second time; and the season of the year might advantage us, and incommode them."

On 21st August, Sir Thomas Fairfax appeared with his army before Bristol, and on that and the following days the siege was formed, and for some days afterwards the soldiers of Fairfax were occupied in preliminary work in trenches, and in repulsing the almost daily sallies which were made by the garrison.

The slow operations of a siege, however, were unsuited to the dispositions of Fairfax and Cromwell, and at a Council of war, held on the 2nd September, it was unanimously resolved that the city should be taken by storm.

Before resorting to this step Fairfax took an unusual and remarkable course—after summoning Prince

Rupert to surrender, he thus continued—" I wish it may be as effectual with you as it is satisfactory to myself that I do a little expostulate with you about the surrender of the city, which I confess is a way not common, and which I should not have used, but in respect to such a person and such a place. I take into consideration your Royal birth and relation to the Crown of England, your honour, courage, and the virtue of your person, and the strength of that place which you may think yourself bound and able to maintain." Then followed an argument to prove that Parliament were really fighting in the interest of the Crown, and that the King's worst enemies were the evil councillors who estranged him from his people; and then he added:

"Sir, if God make this clear to you as it is to us, I doubt not but he will give you a heart to deliver this place, notwithstanding all the other considerations of honour, courage, fidelity, &c., because their consistency and use in the present business depend upon the right and wrongfulness of this that hath been said. And if, upon such conviction you should surrender it, and save the loss of blood, or hazard of spoiling such a city, it would be an occasion glorious in itself and joyfull to us, for the restoring of you to the endeared affections of the Parliament and people of England—the truest friends to your family it hath in the world."

"But if this be hid from your eyes, and that through your wilfulness, this so great, so famous, so ancient a city, and so full of people, be, by you, putting us to force the same, exposed to ruin and the extremity of war, which yet we shall in that case as much as possible endeavour to prevent, then I appeal to the righteous God to be judge between you and us, and to requite the wrong."

"And let all England judge whether the burning of its towns, ruining its cities, and destroying its people be a good requital from a person of your family, which hath had the prayers, tears, purses, and blood of its Parliament and its people; and, if you look on either as now divided, which hath ever had the same party both in Parliaments, and amongst the people most zealous for their assistance and restitution, which you now oppose and seek to destroy, and whose constant grief hath been that their desires to serve your family have ever been hindered and made fruitless by that same party about his Majesty, whose councils you act, and whose interest you pursue in this unnatural war."

It is impossible to know whether this appeal made any impression on the mind of Rupert, but it may well have found an echo there. He had now been three years in England, and his track had been marked by ruined cities, plundered homesteads, and desolate hearths; he had earned the bitter curses of the Roundheads, and by far seeing Cavaliers was regarded with suspicion and distrust; he had done his Sovereign no service, and secured nothing for himself. What was to be the issue of the strife? and what the advantage of protracting it? If he held the city for six months where was the army of relief by which the siege could then be raised? The King might relieve Hereford or feast at Ragland—could he collect an army wherewith to baffle Fairfax and Cromwell? and was he, Rupert, to sacrifice the lives of his brave garrison in order to protract for a few months longer a vain defence?

He must have felt the truth of the remonstrance of Fairfax. The men who had striven to uphold his Father's Throne were the Parliament and people of England; the men who had checked their enthusiasm and thwarted their endeavours were the King and the courtiers by whom he was surrounded and led. He must have felt, too, that his own exertions had all been levelled against the friends of his house and name, and that he had thrown in his lot with the men whose assistance might have saved, but whose indifference accomplished the overthrow of his Father and his Father's cause.

The immediate result of the summons of Fairfax was a correspondence with the Prince as to the terms on which the city should be rendered up. Such a negotiation cannot be justified. A few days earlier Rupert pledged himself to maintain Bristol against the enemy for full four months—and now, before a serious blow was struck, before an assault was even menaced, he negotiated for the betrayal of the trust he was bound as a soldier and a gentleman to perform. Neither is the matter rendered less culpable by his own declaration, for one of the statements it contains is, that at the Council of war where resistance was resolved on, the Prince made the following proposal. "His Highness made offer, that, for his own person, he would attempt to break through with his horse, with such officers as could be spared, leaving such as were requisite for the fort and castle. This by all us, the Colonels of Posts and officers, was thought neither safe or honorable. In the second place he offered to put himself on the defence of the castle and fort. All the officers were clear of opinion against this; that, as regards to the nobility and gentry, and such of the town as appeared well affected, and the horse and foot which the fort and castle could not receive, had been thereby left to the sword of the enemy; and in regard the fort and castle, in our opinions, were not tenable against their army."

The correspondence between Fairfax and the Prince was terminated by the former on the 9th September, and he resolved to carry the town by assault on the following day. At two o'clock on the morning of the 10th the assault was accordingly made; it was bravely resisted, and for three hours the Royalists held their ground. At length the weight of numbers prevailed, the Priors Hill Fort, which was the main object of attack, was carried, two of the gates were taken, and the Dragoons of Desborough galloped into the town. Rupert[*] still held the remainder of the forts in the outer line of defences, the whole of the inner line, the castle, and the suburb of Redcliffe; he was not pressed for provisions or ammunition, and could doubtless have held both town and castle for a considerable time. Yet four hours after the capture of Prior's Hill Fort he made overtures for surrender, and after a short negotiation terms were arranged. The garrison was to march out with the honours of war, but the fortifications were to be delivered up intact, the stores were to be handed over, the cannon, ammunition, materials of war, even the very muskets of the soldiers were to pass into the hands of the besiegers, and on such conditions the great city, which for so long had been the principal stronghold of the Crown, opened her gates to the generals and army of the Parliament.

Rupert mistook his position; it was not his province to consider the policy of the defence. Intrusted by the

---

[*] Markham's Fairfax, p. 252.

King with great command he had one only duty, and was bound by every consideration of gratitude and military fidelity to perform it rigidly. That duty was to hold Bristol to the last, and if he had possessed one tithe of the steady resolution his brilliant courage promised, Fairfax might have been kept at bay for months. The chances of defending the castle and some of the forts were at least equal to those of Massey when the siege of Gloucester was formed; had they been a hundred-fold less favourable the hopelessness of his position could not have altered the duty of the Prince. Nevertheless Bristol was surrendered, and Rupert gallantly arrayed rode out of the abandoned city; his banners were flying, his drums were beating, and all the state and circumstance of war adorned that melancholy pageant. Rupert marched out of Bristol, and of all that was his, left there nothing save honour.

The terrible and unexpected tidings reached the astonished King. Bristol had fallen, yet Rupert lived and was unharmed. The man who had rendered himself conspicuous by reckless courage had turned craven; the Nephew indebted to him for rank, favour, and countless benefits had betrayed him; the Councillor in whom he trusted had proved false to every promise, and deserted his Master when he might have saved the Crown.

At the side of Charles stood his evil genius. Digby, afterwards Lord Bristol, was the secret enemy of Rupert; for months he had plotted his ruin, and now the misconduct of the Prince and his own fortune, enabled him to accomplish it. He used his varied powers to persuade the King he was betrayed, and, without affording opportunity for explanation or time for argument,

Charles dismissed his Nephew from all his employments and commands.

Simultaneously with this hasty sentence, the King wrote a letter to Rupert which expressed in noble language his bitterness and grief. It was worthy the occasion and the man, and is one of a series of documents which would have stamped their author as the ablest writer of the age, even if the tragic interest which surrounds his story had not partially disarmed criticism and softened political wrath.

" Nepheu,

" Though the loss of Bristol be a great blow to me, yet your surrendring it as you did, is of so much affliction to me, that it makes me forget not only the consideration of that place, but is lykewaies the greatest tryall of my constancy that hath yet befalen me; for what is to be done after one, that is so neer me as you ar, both in blood and friendship, submits himself to so meane an action? (I give it the easiest term) Such * * * * I have so much to say, that I shall say no more of it: only, lest rashness of judgment be layed to my charge, I must remember you of your letters of the 12th of August, whereby you assured me (that if no mutiny hapned,) you would keep Bristol for fower months. Did you keep it fower days? Was there anything like mutiny? More questions might be asked, but now, I confesse to little purpose. My conclusion is, to desyre you to seek your subsistence untill it shall please God to determine my condition somewhere beyond seas; to which end I send you herewith a passe, and I pray God to make you sensible of your present condition, and give you means to redeme what you had lost; for I shall have no greater joy in a victory, than a just occasion without blushing to assure you of my being

"Your loving Oncle and most
"Faithful Friend
"CHARLES R.
"Hereford, 14th Sept. 1645."

A letter from the King to Secretary Nicholas dated also Hereford, the 14th September, proves that he thought his Nephew had betrayed him. It enclosed copies of his letters, a warrant to arrest Colonel Legge, the Governor of Oxford, who was known to be devotedly attached to Rupert, "and lastlye, a warrant to be directed to what person shall be thought fittest for the appreheninge my Nepheu Rupert, in case of such extreamitye as shall bee hereafter specifyed, and not otherwise * * the warrant for my Nepheu's comitment is onlye that you may have the power to doe it, if instead of submitting to, and obeying my commands in going beyond the sea, you shall find that he practise the raysinge of mutinye or any other disturbance." The King added the following paragraph in a postscript "Tell my Sone that I shall lesse greeve to heere that he is knoked in the head then that he should doe so meane an action as is the rendring of Bristoll Castell & Fort upon the termes it was."

Rupert replied to the King's letter:
"To the King
"Sire,
"I have received both your letters of the same tenor, from Ragland,* September 14th with the other

---

* The letter dismissing Rupert is dated Ragland, September 14th, though the second letter is dated from Hereford. The fact is explained thus :—it appears by the *iter Carolinum* that the King was at Ragland from 11th to the 14th September, on that day the following is the entry "Abergavenny dinner 14th. Sunday the 14th to Monmouth, dinner the Governors; to Hereford supper."

intimations of your pleasure of the same date, which, as far as my power can make them, are already obeyed: my not having any command, or meddling in your service, rendering it very easy for me to comply with your will to have it so; for no other motive or consideration first or last made me an actor but to do you service, and that as you desired. How I have behaved myself, from the beginning until the misfortune of your command engaged me in Bristol, from inferior persons I shall not desire greater justification or applause than that which I have received from your Majesty, wherefore I pass all former times without mention, and come to this; of which I only say, that if your Majesty had vouchsafed me so much patience as to hear me inform you before you had made a final judgment—I will presume to present this much—that you would not have censured me as it seems you do: and that I should have given you as just satisfaction as in any former occasion, though not so happy. But since there is so great appearance that I must suffer that it is already decreed; what otherwise I should have desired to have given your Majesty an account, now I am obliged to seek for my own clearing: that what you will have me bear, may be with as much honour to me as belongs to integrity. If your Majesty will admit me to that opportunity, I desire to wait on you to that end as soon as I can, when I know I have your leave for it, which I humbly desire to have. If I must be so unfortunate not to to be allowed (if since the first duty that I owe, which is to your Majesty, is not suffered me, to perform wherein else I should rest) in the next place I owe myself that justice as to publish to the world what I think will clear my erring, in all this business now in question, from any foul deed or neglect, and vindicate me from your desert of any prevailing malice, though I suffer it. Your commands that I should dispose of myself somewhere beyond seas, be pleased to consider of, whether it be in my power (though you have sent me a pass) as times now are, to go by it. Wherever I am, or how unhappy so ever, and by your will made so, yet I ever retain that duty to your Majesty which I have ever as

"Your Majesty's most humble, and most
obedient Nephew, and faithful humble servant,
"RUPERT.
"September, 1645."

The letter of Rupert was not couched in courtly language, but it correctly portrayed the state of his haughty and ungoverned spirit. He had right on his side when he complained of being condemned unheard and demanded an enquiry into his conduct, but the taunts with which his remonstrance and demand were mingled sat ill on the partizan who had endangered his Uncle's Crown. Perhaps the Royal pass was no longer available in an outport; but it was not for the man who rendered up the last and most important of them thus to reproach his Sovereign with its loss. Possibly if his demand had been refused him, he might justly have prepared and published the vindication of which his letter spoke; until that refusal had been given, he had no right to menace the King with such a step.

Rupert determined to seek Charles and win from his justice or fears a retractation of the stigma cast upon him—but where was the King from 7th September to 14th October? When he finally reached Newark, he had wandered from Ragland to Chirk, from Hereford to

Chester, amid the mountains of Wales, across the broad plain of Shropshire, thence back again to where the stately castle towered above the rapid Severn and the terraced houses of Bridgnorth, and then, turning Eastward, rested for a while in the Close of Lichfield.

"Often," says Mr. Disraeli,* "the King rode hard through the night, and saw the break of day, which only recalled the weary fugitive to the anxious cares of a retreat, or a pursuit. Once, late in the evening, the King summoned several gentlemen together, and after their conference, he dismissed them to their beds with this pathetic address, "Gentlemen! go you and take your rest, for you have houses and homes, and beds to lodge in, and families to love and live with—but I have none! My horse is waiting for me to travel all this night, and return to the place whence I came." The King had long been like a hunted partridge flitting from one ground to another—this is an affecting image given of his erratic and anxious courses."

After many wanderings Charles had reached Newark. That town was conveniently placed either for a retreat on Oxford, or for a march Northward, should the King determine on a junction with Montrose. Rupert resolved to go there, and fought his way with a troop of Officers and attendants to Belvoir Castle. When Charles heard of his Nephew's approach, he wrote a letter to him requiring him "to stay at Belvoir" till further orders, and reprehending him for not having given obedience to his former commands." Nevertheless, the Prince persevered, and the Garrison of Newark with Sir Richard Willis, the Governor, accompanied by Lord Gerrard and a hundred horse

---

* Disraeli' Commentaries on the Life of Charles I., vol 5, p. 103, edit. 1831.

rode two miles out of the town to welcome him. With scanty courtesy, and none of that ceremonious observance which his duty to the King should have exacted from him, Rupert forced himself into the Royal presence, and stated he had come to account for the loss of Bristol.

Charles, justly offended at the conduct of Rupert, barely acknowledged his presence, and spoke but little to him, and then His Majesty, says Sir Edward Walker, went to supper, Prince Rupert and his brother standing by, his Majesty addressing himself in discourse to Prince Maurice. On the following day however, the King granted a Council of War, and the resolutions then arrived at are embodied in the document, dated March ·21st October, 1645, (No. 27). The finding of the Council was deemed a triumph by the adherents of Rupert, yet it went no further than to pronounce that he had shewn no want courage and fidelity, it did not acquit him of the gravest indiscretion or want of judgment, excused the errors of his military career at the expense of his intellect, and pronounced him at the same time a loyal and incompetent captain.

The King, whose position at Newark was perilous, resolved to leave the town. He had, however, been there long enough to know that Sir Richard Willis and his Officers had committed great excesses, that they had treated the neighbourhood as an enemy's country, and were regarded with hatred and fear by those who would under other circumstances have been devoted to his cause. The Royal Commissioners who comprised the principal gentlemen of the county round were alienated, they had performed their difficult duty with fidelity and zeal, but they could not be expected to persevere in their efforts if their property and dependents were to be at the mercy of an insolent soldiery and their pampered chiefs. Charles resolved to commit the town to other and more trustworthy keeping, and he informed Willis, with many gracious expressions intended to break his fall, that he was on the eve of quitting Newark, and that (as he proposed to raise him to the position of Captain of his Horse Guards, in place of the Earl of Lichfield, recently slain at Chester) he would take him with him, leaving Lord Bellasis as governor in his room.

Willis remonstrated, but in vain, and then withdrew from the presence chamber. In a short time however, he gathered about him the Palatine Princes, Lord Gerrard, and others of their faction, and accompanied by them again forced himself on the attention of the King. Prince Rupert said that Willis was dismissed "for no fault that had been committed, but for being his friend"; Lord Gerrard denounced Digby as a traitor, and said he had instigated the step now taken, while Willis himself, whom the King wished to speak with apart, refused to follow him, declaring that he had received a public injury, and therefore that he expected a public satisfaction.

The malcontents aroused the slumbering passion of the King. Misfortune had dogged his steps, he was flying from his enemies, he had few indeed on whom he could rely, but he disdained to submit to insults in his own presence chamber, or endure from officers who held his commission insolence greater than he had ever yet experienced from those who fought against him.

Charles had almost unexampled self-control; the news of the murder of Buckingham had not disturbed his devotions, the intelligence that he was betrayed did not prevent him from finishing a game of chess—but now, remembering he was a King, he regarded the men before him with deep resentment, and commanded them to depart from his presence and enter it no more.

They left him, yet made one more effort to change his resolution. They presented a remonstrance, desiring that those of them who were deemed unworthy or incapable should be tried by a Council of War, and that if the charges against them were disproved, the King " would grant them either reparation in honour against their enemies or liberty to pass into other parts." Clarendon* states that in presenting this remonstrance the petitioners said, " they hoped his Majesty would not look upon this action of theirs as a mutiny." The King answered " he would not christen it; but it looked very like one. As to the Court of War he would not make that a judge of his actions, but for the papers they should be immediately prepared for as many as desired to have them."

There must have been sad hearts as the trumpets of Prince Rupert sounded to horse, and at the head of some 200 gentlemen he turned his back upon his uncle, and slowly rode away. There must have been much of anger, of bitterness, of offended pride in the men who followed him; some of them had faithfully served their King from the commencement of the troubles, with courage and fidelity, though not always with wisdom and success; most of them had risked all that they had to lose on the issue of the war; among their ranks was many a man of great possessions and ancient name—and now they must wander forth into the world exiles and adven-

---

* Clarendon Vol. 5, p. 295, 360. Warburton Vol. 3, p. 200. Et seq.

turers, without fortune, without employment, without even the favour of the Sovereign for whom they had made these sacrifices, to seek a precarious subsistance as mercenaries in foreign armies, or pensioners at foreign Courts.

And he, too, the deserted King, beset by advancing armies, a fugitive, yet hesitating to leave the sheltering walls around him, what must have been his reflections as his alienated subjects marched forth? Now, more than ever, he needed Rupert's fiery courage and decision of purpose; he ill could spare the soldierly qualities, the ability and the fidelity, as yet untainted, of Sir R. Willis,* and he must have thought with some bitterness of the unstable Gerrard, so recently ennobled by, yet so promptly to abandon him.

Rupert marched to Belvoir Castle, and from that stronghold despatched Lieutenant-Col. Osborne, on 29th October, with a letter addressed to "the Lords and Commons in Parliament assembled." In this letter he stated that he and the Officers and Gentlemen with him were "altogether disengaged from the service," they had been in, and asked a pass and safe convoy for them to go abroad or return to their houses." The letter from Col. Osborne of 1st November (No. 25) was followed by a second letter on the same day, in which he detailed at great length the difficulties with which negociations were attended,† and finally when the pass was granted, it was conditional on the Prince and his friends pledging themselves not to serve the King again, and they refused to accept it. They then fought their way to Woodstock,

---

* Sir R. Willis, during the Protectorate, betrayed the Royalists plans to Cromwell.—Clarendon v. 7, p. 234. See also Thurloe's State papers, Vol. 1.
† Warburton, Rupert and Cavaliers, Vol. 3, p. 210.

where they remained a considerable time in sullen inaction, doing nothing for the King and very little for their own benefit.

The letter No. 29 must have been written between 1st November 1645 and January 1st 1646, but there is nothing to shew who was the author of it. It is endorsed as being undated and unsigned, and we gather from the context that the writer was a sincere friend of Rupert and had access to the King. It was one of a series of letters breathing the same sentiments which were addressed to the Prince from various quarters, and there is a pathos about it which might well impress a hasty and generous nature. The ties of blood were highly reverenced in that age, and the writer might fairly urge that Rupert could not degrade himself by submitting to one to whom he owed an almost filial duty Then too the allusion to the fallen condition of the royal cause, "a King not in a condition he merryt" was full of sad and melancholy meaning; for many months there had been no rift in the dark and lowering clouds which had gathered round the unhappy Charles; city, town, and fortress had been rendered up on conditions, or been pitilessly stormed, and the sentinels of the rebels were pacing the ramparts of Chester, and the weeds were growing over the site of Basing House. While this ruin was being worked Rupert was playing with his sword knot, and indulging in sullen discontent. Was this slothworthy the impetuous Cavalier who scarcely three years ago had been the hope of his party, and the stay of his Uncle's throne? Was it worthy of the hero before whose headlong charge the soldiers of the Parliament had never stood their ground? And above all had he a right to contribute to the ruin of his friends, who could not in honour submit to the King so long as he stood aloof.

In the same strain as this anonymous correspondent the faithful and honourable William Legge addressed the Prince, "You should write to your Uncle * * you ought to do it, and if you offer your service to him yet, and submit yourself to his disposing and advice, many of your friends think it could not be a dishonour, but rather the contrary, seeing he is a King, your Uncle, and in effect a parent to you." The Earl of Dorset wrote thus, "If my prayers can prevail, you shall not have the heart to leave us all in our saddest times; and if my advice were worthy of following, truly you should not abandon your Uncle in the disastrous condition his evil stars have placed him. Let your resolution be as generous and great as is your birth and courage. Resolve, Princely Sir, to sink or swim with the King; adjourn all particular respect or interest until the public may give way to such unlucky disputes."

Yielding at length to these entreaties the Prince submitted himself to his Uncle—he acknowledged "the great error which happened on the occasion of Newark," he protested that love and affection to his service had ever really been in his heart, and he beseeched the King to dispose of him in the way be thought most fit.

A submission so unqualified would have satisfied a sterner man than Charles, even had it proceeded from a partizan of lesser note. In this instance, however, many circumstances combined to make his forgiveness sincere; in his secret musings he might well reproach himself for his conduct to his sister; he might well reflect that ties of blood, and political interest and the cause of his religion had all appealed to him in her favour, and appealed in vain; he might well remember that the high offices he had conferred upon Rupert had been justified, if they had not been earned, by his zeal, his fidelity, and his abounding courage.

He might have acknowledged to himself the faults his Nephew had committed were those of a noble nature irritated by failure, goaded into excesses by machinations of secret foes, and thrown off its balance by aspersions fatal to his own honour and that of his most trusted friends. The anxious outlook of the future must also have influenced the King as the sanguine hopes that had beguiled him, one by one faded away. Montrose was a fugitive; Digby had been ignominiously routed; and every day made it more apparent that in advising a reconciliation with the Parliament, Rupert had counselled him unselfishly and well. The letter which Charles had addressed to his Nephew many months previously shows that even then he saw nothing but ruin in the future, and the warning of calamity which fate thus give him must have made him anxious while there was yet time to welcome Rupert back again to his confidence and regard.

The Prince was again at the right hand of the King, but other advisers had now their Sovereign's ear; and when Charles left Oxford to throw himself on the calculating generosity of the Scotch covenanters, he went against the advice of Rupert, and accompanied only by Ashburnham and Dr. Hudson.

And now the struggle which for four years had devastated England was over. The Scotch surrendered Charles to the Parliament; the loyal garrisons everywhere were commanded by the King to make terms and abandon their fortresses; Newark the scene of such eventful incidents was surrendered, and the fortifications were razed; the gates of impregnable Oxford were thrown open to Fairfax and his soldiers; and soon there was not a city or a fortress which did not acknowledge the authority of the Parliament*

The letter of Charles II. to Prince Rupert dated 18th December is endorsed by Colonel Bennett as having been probably written in 1653.

For some years after the Royal cause was lost in England Rupert led a life of strange and adventurous daring; ready to engage in any quarrel, willing to hazard the lives of himself and his friends on behalf of any one who would hire his aid, he seemed the imitator and successor of the free lance of an earlier age. During this period of his life one phase of it was his career at sea. By force, by argument, or cajolery he succeeded in obtaining some ships belonging to the English navy, styled himself Admiral, and became in reality a pirate. His ideas of friend and foe were confused—his theories as to what was a fair prize were directly governed by his interests, and he won a fitful and fluctuating income at the expense, in the main, of Englishmen.

---

* The following letter was written by Charles.

Hudson not having time, I desire you to advertise all the several loyal governors of my remaining towns and forts, that I wish them now to make their compositions upon the best terms they may, for the truth is I cannot relieve them; but assure them, that as their suffering is my greatest affliction so, whensoever God shall enable me, they shall reap the fruits of their fidelity, nor shall grief ever go from my heart until I have shewn by my successful actions that I am to you all

A really constant friend,

CHARLES R.

Newcastle, 18th Jan. 1646.

When he had money at command he gave a portion of it to Charles II., and that King, without a Throne, thus shared the plunder and benefitted by the injuries inflicted on his subjects.

In the beginning of 1653 Rupert landed at Nantes. Of all his ships he brought only one maimed vessel into port and she, too, perished a few days later. He had, however, made various prizes and conveyed their contents to shore. The Parliament remonstrated against the countenance shewn the Prince by France, but his acheivements had pleased the fancy of Louis XIV. and instead of listening to their complaints he made him Master of the Horse.

In the meantime Charles was a troublesome and dangerous guest, there was scanty honour and no advantage to be gained by his presence, and the French King wished him to remove to other lands. A Pretender may often be a useful ally, but a Pretender who had exhausted all his powers of offence in vain, who had become simply an object of sorrow to his friends and derision to his enemies, was a useless burthen at the Court of the magnificent and ambitious Louis. Too proud to drive the exile from his presence he yet intimated to him his desire that he should depart, and placed at his command funds sufficient to enable him to act upon the suggestion. Charles apparently spent the pistoles and remained in Paris.

In Thurloe's State papers there are letters which bear on the present condition of affairs. After the Prince was appointed Master of the Horse we are told that he returned to Nantes, and " made a good bargain for his sugars."

"Prince Rupert is gone to Nantes, and some say his cause of leaving the town was, that they were here to make a process against him for all the prizes he took at sea from all kinds of Merchants, without exception, which he sold in several places in France, without any licence from his Majesty of France. King Charles intended for Holland, and from thence to Denmark. What shall be the end of his designs I do not yet know."*

Another account from the same source is as follows :—

"The titular King of England received money for his journey into Holland * * * * What should his excellency my Lord General Cromwell expect from the Cardinal but a parcel of fair promises in answer to his letter? I assure the King and Cardinal are resolved not to deliver Prince Rupert's merchandizes, what language soever or fair words they give you. His mind is at rest, there is such assurances given by the Queen, Cardinal, and Council, I protest they laugh at you, and think your demands so insolent, as nothing more. In the English Court, though there are but few poor Ministers and Lords, there is as much confusion as ever was at the Tower of Babylon."†

No condemnation of that frivolous and licentious Court could be too severe; three or four men, such as Hyde and Nicholas, were far seeing, faithful and devoted; the others were gamblers and debauchees, men of loose principles and unstable purposes, whose word no man would take and in whose honour no woman could confide.

---

* Thurloe's State Papers, 388, Paris, 9th August 1653 (U.S.)
† A letter of intelligence from Paris, 19th July 1653. Thurloe's State Papers, Vol. I, p. 344.

The private letters of the period which their authors supposed would never see the light, disclose the character and pursuits of Charles. Thus for example, Sir Richard Browne, writing to Hyde on 15th November 1653, says, " finding that some moneys of his Maties will remaine with me, I humbly submitt it to your Hon^{rs} consideration whether a hundred Lewises in gold will not be acceptable to his Ma^{ty} to be by your Hon^r privately delivered into his owne Royall hands, towards his merry playing, wherwith to passe his time at cards this approaching Christmasse." And the grave and prudent Clarendon thus replies to the proposal, which in effect was intended to bribe the King out of his own monies—the Chancellor of the Exchequer however knew his master, and we blame him not for accepting as a gift an offering which might well have been resented as an insult. " I cannot," he says, " but commende your designe, and as I believe the Kinge does not expecte such a present, so I am sure it will be most wellcome to him, and I will promise you to present it to him, in so secrett a manner, as nobody shall know it but himselfe; and be confident I will never converte one penny that belonges to him, to my owne use, in what straights soever I should be."

The same correspondence discloses the pecuniary difficulties of Hyde. Sir Richard Browne had written to tell him he had sent him some wine of which a portion was intended for Lady Lucas, and the letter from which we have already quoted is written in reply to this intimation—it thus continues—" I like very well your distribution of the sacke, and I will not bragge of my share, nor fayle of delivering the proportion you assigne, and if the good lady comes hither, (as by yours I guesse she intends to do, though Paris at present is a place of prod'gious exspence. every thinge double the pryse of what it was when you left it) the vessell shall stay with her; and I then shall be sure of justice, and I will fetch my allowance in bottles: Let me only give you this warninge, that the carriage be payd for, as I thinke you told me in your former that it was, and I am sure I cannot do it, and then, the sooner it comes the better."

On 27th December following Hyde thus acknowledges an offer of money from Browne. "For your new noble offer. I am not in a condition so plentiful to refuse, for I must tell you I have not had a Lewis of my owne these three months; therefore when you send the bill, lett me know whether you lend me so much oute of your owne little stocke, or whether it be the King's money, for in that case his Ma^{ty} shall be the disposer, since my office hath never yett nor shall intitle me to take his money without his direction."

Meanwhile in utter loneliness of heart and aim, surrounded by secret enemies, by hesitating friends, and an awe struck people, Cromwell pursued his solitary and determined way. His character and career have been made the mark in our own days of ill considered and fulsome panegyric; writers who never acknowledge merit until success has crowned her efforts, have recognized in this great man every virtue required to make up their ideal of perfection. We enter not into the controversy; but we see in his stern concentration of purpose, the relentless energy with which he trampled down every obstacle that barred his way to power, and the vast sway he exercised over a fanatical and devoted army, qualities which belong only to men whose ability is guided by unbending resolution, and a clear idea of the ends they seek. Since the execution of his King Cromwell must have regarded with deep contempt the conduct of the Parliament—by the aid of the weapon he had forged and placed in their hands, they had destroyed the Monarchy, abolished the Upper House, and replaced Laud, Juxon and the Clergy of the Establishment, by a crowd of obscure and illiterate Ministers—but, powerful as they were to destroy, what had they created, what were the institutions they proposed to substitute for those which they had swept away, and with what breakwater did they intend to check the angry tide of discontent which was gradually rising and threatened to overwhelm them.

Within a few hours of the time when Charles wrote his letter to Prince Rupert, Cromwell was proclaimed Protector; he bound himself by solemn oaths to maintain the constitution then established; he received the homage of state and army; and the long line of English Monarchs was apparently swept away for ever to make room for military usurpation. Much wisdom was evinced in the ordinances then established; many anomalies were abolished; many an ancient chamber was swept and garnished; the changes in the representative system might, had they been persisted in, have prevented the long struggle for reform which the present and past generation has witnessed, and the tolerance accorded, with two exceptions, to every form of Christian belief was wise, far seeing, and unparalleled.

There were blots in the rule of Cromwell, and he was guilty of tyranny and oppression. His government, however. was free from the vacillation of Charles I. and the paltry vices of his son; at least it gave England "peace at home and triumph abroad," and made his subjects feel like the Roman of ancient days that wherever they wandered a far seeing eye and an all-protecting arm watched over their interest and ensured their safety.

Whatever were the faults of Cromwell he never degraded his country. He never abandoned the Protestant cause like Charles I., or sold himself to France like his successor. With few attributes that could command the love or attract the sympathy of his countrymen, he was free from the vices which before and after him made legitimate Monarchs the objects of the misgiving and scorn of those even who wished them well.

The restoration of Charles II. was the natural sequence of the Commonwealth, the Protectorate, and the anarchy that threatened England when Cromwell died. Theorists of all kinds had experimented on their country, and their experiments had failed; the foreign triumphs of the Protector had not been greater than those won by a woman a hundred years before; the peace at home which England enjoyed was precarious, troubled and broken; it was the peace of exhaustion not of content, and beneath its unruffled surface the conspirator plotted, while the patriot mourned.

Twenty years of strife, destruction, and repression had passed, and men asked themselves with what result. The great institutions reared centuries before had crumbled into dust; the Crown was gone with all its splendid pageantries, and all its historic claims; the Church was swept away, and in the defaced temples of happier times Fifth Monarchy men prophesied and

Ranters raved; the great families, who had a lasting hold on the affections of the multitude, were exiled, disgraced, or shorn of half their property; in their place new men ruled who had no sympathy with the people round them, and made no allowance for their weakness and faults; a spirit of fanaticism and gloomy intolerance brooded over the land; every amusement which made life cheerful to the peasant, or graceful and refined to his superiors was repressed as sinful, or sneered at as profane; and all this while the citizen was weighed down by unaccustomed taxation to provide pay for an army which he detested and feared.

There was the stain of blood on the robe of Cromwell which he had neither time nor opportunity to efface. A stern soldier, a remorseless conqueror, a despot in act, and ruling by despotic agencies, while feared by everyone, he was despised by half England as an upstart, and hated by the other half as a tyrant. The men who endeavoured to succeed him had all his faults, but were without the great qualities by which they were so nearly atoned. If they had had the daring and the good fortune to take his place they would only have exhibited on a grand theatre the miserable spectacle of their own incapacity and folly; while the Parliament which was in England their competitor for power was the same effete and despised convention which Cromwell years since had dissolved, amid sympathetic jeers and execrations from a gazing populace.

In every class therefore men were to be found whose prejudices, feelings, and interests were hostile to the existing order of affairs, and they looked back with regret to the institutions that had been subverted, to the men who were in exile and their youthful King.

It was under the influence of these feelings that Charles II. was welcomed home. A sceptic in religion, a profligate in conduct, trusting in no one, believing in the sanctity of no cause, he yet was hailed as the representative of order, the guardian of the Church, the heir of a sacred and ancient throne. How he disappointed every hope that his friends and his loyal subjects cherished; how he sacrificed his people's good and his own dignity on the altar of degraded passion, it is not our province to trace; the task would be long and irksome, and would chronicle the progress of national disgrace, and the weary record of national decay. We are concerned not with the history of the Reign of Charles II. but with the condition of affairs 19 years subsequently to the restoration, and in a few paragraphs we will endeavour to depict it.

In the first burst of loyalty which welcomed the King to his own again, the convention was dissolved, and a new Parliament summoned. It assembled on 8th May 1661, and reflected with great fidelity the momentary passions of the people. Every where the Roundheads and sectaries were discomfited, the men who had suffered in person and estate for their loyalty were elected, and the assembly which then for the first time met was rightly called the Cavalier Parliament.

The work of 20 years was undone in one—the Church was re-established; the King was endowed with every power and prerogative his Father wielded; the Regicides were sent to scaffold or dungeon; and England regarded the Commonwealth and Protectorate as a hideous dream, from which, in a fortunate moment she had been aroused.

Yet men still lived who had perilled life and fortune in the cause which now seemed so forlorn, and they watched with patient constancy till the principles they believed were eternal should again be recognised as true. Their chosen ministers perished day by day in the prisons of the Priests of Baal—the high places of this world were filled with the licentious Rochester, the persecutor Clarendon, the apostate Shaftesbury, and other men more worthless still, while the King and his Courtiers lived lives of open profanity, scoffing at the most sacred human ties, and violating the solemn ordinances of God. The stern sectary, the honest enthusiast, and the ardent advocate of freedom, watched these things and regarded the present as a time of trial and persecution, while they believed a brighter day would dawn ere long, and that the principles which had so lately been in the ascendant, though suffering from momentary eclipse, would shine forth again in splendour and illuminate the regenerated land.

There was also a large party professing royalist opinions, who, as time went on, regarded with unconcealed digust the vices of the Court. These men felt now that the struggle of twenty years was over, that the very principles they had striven for were set at nought. They had fought for the Crown and its prerogatives, but not for uncontrolled power guided by frivolity and vice; for a Church which Laud with all his faults had sought to regenerate, and not for a shameless hierarchy whose only idea of duty was to preach the right divine, and pander to the vices of the Crown; they had been earnest for the Protestant cause, using that word in its widest sense, and were unprepared for the altered policy which was leading the nation to Rome.

A few more years passed by and these feelings became deeper and more widely spread. The foreign policy of Charles was shameful and ignominious. The Dutch fleet sailed in triumph up the Thames, Dunkirk was sold for money, and French gold supplied the funds required for the debaucheries of the King.

Gradually too, as far as any policy could be pursued by that unstable and frivolous nature, it became evident that Charles intended to govern unshackled by precedent or law. His ideas of royal power were based on the model of the French Court, and he resolved, as opportunity offered itself, to curb the freedom which was now trammelling him. His encroachments were, it is true, fitful and wayward, but they all tended in the same direction, the suppression of the liberties of England.

It was not only the civil liberties of his subjects that were menaced by the King, it was also his intention to reconcile England with the Papal see; the work which cost James his Crown, was stealthily commenced by Charles, and was carried on by him as opportunity offered, or caprice enjoined. These efforts were concealed as far as possible from the knowledge of the people, but rumours of them spread abroad and created suspicion and widespread alarm.

It was at the time when the fears of the people were at their height that two circumstances tended to increase them. The first of these was the infamous fabrication of Titus Oates, the second the conduct of Ashley Cooper, Lord Shaftesbury. The character and career of Oates are so generally understood that it is needless to advert to them here. It is difficult to fathom the depths of human credulity, and example after example seems to prove that these depths are still unprobed—yet the clumsy fabrications of this illiterate pretender were so palpably false that we wonder that men in power should lend them their passing aid. The spirit of that age was unscrupulous, and Shaftesbury was conspicuous for ability and tergiversation beyond all his contemporaries. He had been disgraced and sent to the Tower, and he resolved to rise again at any cost, and when he was at liberty, with a laugh and a sneer, he took up the story of Oates and the advocacy of the Protestant cause.

Then ensued that memorable and shameful panic in which so many noble lives were lost, and so many spotless reputations were, for the moment, tarnished. The people were mad with superstition and alarm, and, urged by such impulses, were merciless. Circumstances which to this day are unexplained gave to the wildest tales, the most improbable conjectures, the appearance of consistency and truth, and in a paroxysm of frenzy both houses of Parliament resolved that " there hath been and still is a damnable and hellish plot, contrived and carried on by the popish recusants, for assassinating the King, for subverting the government, and for rooting out and destroying the protestant religion."

Oates was lodged in Whitehall, was pensioned, styled the saviour of the nation, his vile utterances were eagerly listened to, and on his evidence men of honour and loyalty were sent to the prison and the block.

In this time of popular excitement, when all England was ringing with the tidings of the great plot, the King resolved to dissolve his Parliament.* It was a strange time at which to have recourse to such a measure, for no man used to public affairs could have failed to see the issue of it. The country, fevered from one end to the other by dangers menacing alike its religion and freedom, was now to be convulsed in every county and every borough by a contest mainly turning on these very perils. A parliament which at its inception had been almost ridiculously loyal, and which was still in the main compliant to the royal will, was to be dissolved at the moment when the shameless traffic with France had been divulged, and the people were writhing under national humiliation and domestic tyranny. Strange, however, as was the moment selected for the dissolution, the motives for it lie on the surface; Charles, as usual, required money and hoped to obtain it from the liberality of new men; he wanted to stay the impeachment of Danby, an impeachment which would have exposed the whole of his shameless intrigues with France, and the only way in which to do so effectually was to dissolve the Parliament by which it had been commenced.

Charles had never been misled by the popular cry, he was too shrewd an observer, and had too sceptical a nature to credit the gross absurdities of Oates and his imitators; yet it was politic to affect a belief he did not feel, and he placed himself unreservedly in the hands of Shaftesbury, jested, and signed death warrants.

The speech from the throne was delivered in person, and Charles announced that he had excluded the Popish Lords from Parliament, that he had sanctioned

---

*Parliament was prorogued on 30 Decr. 1678, dissolved on 24 Jany. 1679 and the new Parliament assembled and the royal speech was delivered on 6th March, 1679.

"the execution of several men, both on the score of the Plot, and the murder of Sir Edmundbury Godfrey, and it is apparent," he added, "that I have not been idle in prosecuting the discovery of both, as much farther as hath been possible in so short a time · · and above all I have commanded my brother to absent himself from me, because I would not leave malicious men room to say, I had not removed all causes which could be pretended to influence me towards Popish Counsels."*

This Parliament was in turn dissolved, as is stated in the letter from William Bennett of that date, on 10th July following, and the new Parliament was summoned to assemble on 17th October. In the meanwhile a sudden illness of the King alarmed his Councillors. and the Duke of York was hastily summoned from Brussels so as to be on the spot.

In the following October, Charles resolved to send the Duke of York to Scotland, as it was thought he could conciliate that Kingdom where the Covenantors had been cruelly repressed by Monmouth and Claverhouse.† It was also supposed that his presence there would gain adherents to his cause in the event of a struggle for the succession, ensuing on the death of the King. The letter of William Bennett, of 20th October, relates to the reception of the Duke in the City, immediately before his departure for Scotland.

On 10th January, 1681, the King again dissolved the Parliament, and summoned a new one to meet him in

---

* History and proceedings of the House of Commons from the Restoration to the present time. Vol I. p. 324, Lond : 1742.
† Burnets own times, vol. I, p. 477. edit. 1724.

INTRODUCTION.

Oxford, on 21st March following,* and it is to the election for Shaftesbury, on this occasion that the letters of William Bennett mainly relate. These letters are addressed to Colonel Benett, of Norton Bavant, Wilts, who was elected Member for Shaftesbury, in the year 1679. At the poll held on 13th September in that year, the four Candidates for the Borough polled the following nnmber of votes.

Sir Mathew Andrews, Knight	... 268
Thomas Benett	... 218
John Bowles	... 121
Henry Whitaker	... 49

on the present occasion it appears by the correspondence that Colonel Benett was returned at the head of the poll. The politics he professed can be gathered from the fact stated by William Bennett, that Mr. Gray had received a letter from Lord Shaftesbury, stating he was a fit person to represent the town; we therefore assume he was returned as one of the Protestant party of that day, and that it was as a supporter of the men who upheld the exclusive bill, and believed in the popish plot that he earned his title of " honest Tom Benett."

Colonel Benett was, however, something more than the mere dupe of Oates and his gang of fellow conspirators. He was secretary to Prince Rupert, and in the accounts rendered by Lord Craven, the executor to the Prince, one of the largest item is the payment to " Thomas Benett, the secretary, in full of all demands of eight hundred pounds."

In concluding these notices, we have only to add

---

* Rapin vol. ii, p. 595, edit. 1760.

that the documents now printed are in possession Mr. Benett Stanford, the collateral descendant of Colonel Benett, and present member for Shaftesbury. The papers were accidentally discovered by him two years since whilst destroying a vast accumulation of old unarranged and useless documents. In committing these papers to the flames he remarked on one of them the signature "Charles R," and reserved the bundle in which it was contained for further investigation—subsequently the remainder of the documents in his possession were very carefully examined, and the result has been the selection for publication of these which are now printed. Without claiming for them any great historical value, it is yet thought that they possess an interest for the scholar and historian which renders them worthy of publicity, while the domestic letters, and the sketch of a contested election two centuries ago abound in curious details which are not readily met with in other works.

LETTERS.

[No. 1.]

NEPHEU*

I have snached this litle tyme to congratulat your victory asseuring you that this (as the rest) is the welcomer because of you the cheefe Actor. So desyring you to have care of the Armes and Clothes there and thereabouts. I rest   Your loving Oncle and faithfull frend

Oxford 3 Feb.   CHARLES R.
   1642/3

And Mony must not be forgotten.

[No. 2.]

NEPHEU

I send you herewith a proposition concerning Lancasheere with wch I am very much pleased, but I will not conclude it without your advyce; wherefore I desyre you as soone as you can (for this buisness would not be delayed) to let me know your opinion of it, & if you approve it to send my Lord Biron (to whom, only, I desyre you to comunicat this business) presently to me; if not, then to send your objections against it.   So wishing you good success in all your desynes I rest
    Your loving Oncle & most faithfull frend
                          CHARLES R.

Oxford 4 No. 1643

* This letter refers to the storm of Cirencester. See Introduction, p. ix.

This bearer hath desyred leave of me to goe, for sometyme, to Darbysheer, but I refer him & his reasons to you.

My Lo: Capell sends me word that there are great number of Cattel & other Provisions of Victuals at Stafford wch ar to caried to London

---

[No. 3.]

NEPHEU

Though I know that I need not recomend this bearer to you, yet a frend's remembrance, at no tyme can doe no harme; & with this occasion I cannot but mention two Oxford discourses to you; first it is saide that its impossible so to fortafie Tossiter* that it can be kept without so great a force bothe of Horse and Foote that it will not be worth the paines, & that the Horse wch lyes there will be continually put to such hard dewty, that (in short tyme) they are lyke to be much wasted; wherefor as it is possible that now you may fynde this to be so wch at first you did not belive (no more than I doe yet) & therefor thinke fitt to betake you to some other desyine, so by no means, I would not have you be guyded by our foolishe discourses heere, but doe according to your owen judgement; & certainly that Place is of such consequence that is not to quitted but to eschew verrie great inconveniencies wch I hope ye will not finde: the second is that my Wyfe & I ar treating for a Peace wch you must not heare of: this is a damnable Ley;† the ground of it is that the French Ambasador said by way of discourse not proposition that he hoped I would not shutt my eares to honorable & reasonable propositions if they were ofred to me; but protested against treating

---

* Towcester. † See p. xii. of Introduction.

with those who call themselfes the Parliament though I should desyre him : & I against hearing from any of them except from Essex* as Queene Elizabethe & my Father treated with Tyron being the cheefe Rebell : but upon my credit, you shall have notice of the first overtur (of wch yet there is little apearance) & shall have your word about if any such thing be & so I rest

   Your loving Oncle and most faithfull frend
Oxford 12 No. 1643   CHARLES R.

[No. 4.]

     Oxford 4th March 1644.

NEPHEU

 this by my L Loughborow is the first occasion I have had of wryting to you since ye went, for his business, I refer you to himselfe for the particulars, only this, you shall doe well to encourage him what you may, & in the particular of Belvoir Castell to give him contentment as he desyres if you finde it not prejudicial to my service. As for my Western Orders, I have comanded Digby to give you a particular account of all wch I hope you will approve of, they being in persuance of those grounds which you and I have resolved on. I have lykewaise comanded Will Legg† to give you an account of some things, whereby you will perceave, that I have and will keepe my word with you, in the least particular.

 * Robert Devereux, Earl of Essex, made Lord General of the Forces of the Parliament in 1641. He died 14 Sept., 1646, and by his death removed one of the greatest obstacles to the ambition of Cromwell. See Introduction, p. xlii.

 † Colonel William Legge, known as "honest Will Legge," was the attached and faithful friend of Rupert. He had the courage to give him true and unwelcome advice, and appears to have been the best and most reliable councillor the Prince possessed. He was the ancestor of the present Earl of Dartmouth.

In the last place, I must thanke you for undertaking, so cheerfully so difficult a business as you ar about, there being more than one kynde of Ennemy you ar to deale with & therfor no wonder if you doe not succeed but the more praise if you prosper, howsoever you shall still fynde me to be*

   Your loving Oncle & most faithfull friend
          CHARLES R.

[No. 5.]

NEPHEU

I have this day receaved two letters from you, as for the first (wch concernes your Government) my answer is that I meane not to trust you by halfes, therefor I freely give you leave to chuse your Gouernor of Salop† & thinke no reason that Chessheere should be denyed from your Comand: concerning nether of w^{ch}, yet I have been moved, but when I shall, I asseure you, I shall not be altered : as for the Monie Letters I have comanded Jermin‡ to give you an Answer, as lykewais an account of some other things of the lyke nature: as for Newark, I belive before this, you will have understoad my full directions, wch I hope will not be the lesse powerfull, being the more civill: for an earnest desyre to you is as much as a perremptory comand to others, from

     Your loving Oncle & most
Oxford 12 March   faithfull frend
  1643.   CHARLES R.

* This apparently refers to Rupert's Northern Expedition. See Introduction, p. xii.

† Probably this refers to the appointment of Lord Capel, whose proclamation is dated 3 April, 1643.

‡ Henry Jermyn, created Lord Jermyn in the summer of this year, a favourite of the Queen, and reputed to have been her second husband.

[No. 6.]

Oxford 15 March 1643

NEPHEU

I hope you will be satisfied with the care I have taken concerning the Munition, wch I dout not but you will have in good tyme, & I asseure you that there is nothing wch concerns you wch I will not take as much care as if it wer for aine of my children : I have given so full an answer to my Lo: Jermin concerning all your demands that I need not repeat them to you, only this, you fynde that in every particular & on all occasions you will fynde me to bee

Your loving Oncle & most
faithfull frend
CHARLES R.

I shall not faile to see
you satisfied of the 400*l*
you repaid to my Wyfe

[No. 7.]

Oxford 27 March 1643

NEPHEU

I have this day receaved two letters from you & this is the second that I have written to you; the wch together with a trusty Messenger, is the justifible cause of a short letter wherfor at this tyme wholly referring myselfe to your most honest Servant Montaigue Forest

Your loving Oncle & most
faithfull frend
CHARLES R.

[No. 8.]

Oxford 21 April 1644

NEPHEU

By my Lord Byron you will have had the trew state of my affairs heire whereby you will see the absolute necessety of those supplyes therein demanded, but it is, with a supposition that Manchester* doe joine with Essex (of wch we have had confident information) that so, Waler† at the same tyme may goe into the West, this Army not being able, both to defend thease Garisons (wch cannot be otherwais secured) & follow Waler to secure your Brother Maurice; but if Manchester goe Northeward, then I do not conceave your present assistance of so absolute necessety; wherfor I thinke it necessary to give you this further latitude, that in case you get certaine intelligence that Manchester is gone Northe then I give you leave to Keepe your Boddy intyre; (otherwais I stand to my former demand) & in that case, I offer to your considera- tion, whether you will not rather bend towards Yorkesheere to save my L Newcastll (who is lykely to be in verry great distresse) & to leave the Scots, then to reduce Lancashire; if they bee bothe possible, that of Yorkeshire is certainely of much more consequence; but this is meerely to consult not to comande (as concerning this alternative) wch I asseure you I have & meane to doe, in all cases possible, according to the Places that we ar distant

* The Earl of Manchester, instead of uniting with Essex, marched north, and was General of one of the three armies by which York was besieged, and he commanded the left wing of the Parliamentary forces at Marston Moor. He was deprived of his command by the operation of the self-denying ordinances, and after the Restoration was made Lord Chamberlain. He died in 1671.

† Sir William Waller, M.P. for Andover, Lieutenant-General in the Parliamentary army. Waller was surnamed in the early part of the war William the Conqueror, but subsequently he failed to justify this epithet.

one frome the other: & be confident many men has & shall faire the better for your good estimation, none the worse, amongst whome Colonel Charles Garret* hathe & shall be an instance : & in every thing else you will fynde me to be

Your loving Oncle & most
faithfull friend
CHARLES R.

[No. 9.]

NEPHEU

I have no more to say to you concerning the maine business then I have alreddy written to you, by my Lo: Biron, & by two dispaches since; only I send you, heere inclosed, the best intelligence I have, concerning Northern Affaires (the one I am sure is too trew, the other I believe, as coming from a good hand) that you may the better judge what is fittest for you to doe for my service.

You will alreddy have knowen, by my Lo : Biron, the cause of the mistaking concerning Wasshington,† & desyring to repair it, I offer this expedient, that you would send him & his Regiment hither as part of the 2,000 Foote I have sent for, to you, (supplying Easam with other Men) & then I meane to make him Lieutennant

---

* Charles Gerard, afterwards Lieutenant-General of the Horse in the Royal army; created Baron Gerard of Brandon, Nov. 8, 1645. See Introduction, p. lxi.

† Sir Henry Washington was probably Colonel Washington, who in 1643 succeeded in entering Bristol by assault when that city was besieged by Rupert. The place at which he entered was subsequently known as "Washington's bush." He was subsequently knighted, and served in the Royal army till the end of the war. In 1646 he was appointed Governor of Worcester, which he defended resolutely for three months, and then surrendered on honourable terms. He was of the same family as George Washington the American patriot.

Governour of this Cittie : if you can fynde a better, I shall be glad to take it, for I asseure you he is no more esteemed by you than he is by

     Your loving Oncle & most
      faithfull frend

Oxford 24 Ap   CHARLES R.
 1644

     [No. 10.]

         Malberro 8 Feb.
May it please Y^r High^{es} [1643]

 I know not howe well to give credite to it but there is two gentlemen now comme from Newberie frighted from thence the last nightt by intelligence they had of some of the enemies forces were to come into Newberie invited thither by the townesmen whoe have only reported the plague to bee there to keepe the Kings troopes oute, how slight soever this maye bee, sure I am that disaffected towne can nott bee to much punished by Y^r High^{es} for att my coming from Basingstoke they stopped all our baggage and had detained it butt thatt they hered wee were strong enough to revenge itt. The Sherife of this Countie intendes to bee heer this day to order some things for his Maties services; these S^r are the reasons thatt keepe mee a day longer in this burntt & plundered quarter, to-morrow I shall obey the command I have to remove to Andever & doute not but that sudenly Y^r High^{es} would receave a good accountt concerning the designe thatt thatt is in the weye to

    From Y^r High^{es} most humble faithfull
        Servant
          GRANDISON.*

---

 * William Villiers, Viscount Grandison, Colonel of Horse in the Royal army. See Introduction, p. xv.

[No. 11.]

May it please your moste excellente Majestie,

To give me leave to acquainte you with the presente condition I am in Sr William Brewerton is come downe with fower hundred horse and dragooners and joyned with Sr John Gell att Darbye, who had a thousand dragooners and foote, and the Lorde Greye is att Leicester with five hundred. Theis with (Cavelrie) are drawing all againste my Lord of Chesterfield and my selfe and more they expecte. If I had anie considerable strengthe this Countie would be of greate importance to your Majestie, and I finde the people well inclinde but if I quitte the Countrie all these part are utterlie loste though my Lorde of Chesterfield, the gentlemen with me, and myselfe are resolute to fight itt out to the laste if itt be possible to keepe this place, but wee humblie beseeche your Majestie to comand us speedie aide from Banburie, otherwise wee may be all loste, and your cause suffer, which is more deare to me than the life of

Your humble and loyall
Subjecte & Servant
H. HASTINGS.*

Ashby de la Zouch
    Sunday 15 January
        3 of the Clocke.

Addressed "To his moste excellente Majistie at his Court att Oxenforde humblie presents theis."

---

* Henry Hastings, second son of Henry, fifth Earl of Huntingdon, General of the Royal forces in cos. Leicester, Derby, Nottingham, Lincoln, Rutland, and Stafford: created Baron of Loughborough, Oct. 23, 1643. See Introduction, p. xxxii.

[No. 12.]

Sir

I reckon it a greate blessing that you are soe neere us for your fame getts creditt to your Servants and since the report only of your aproaching wee have prospered much; but to compleat our hopes when you come amongst us, I shall make noe doubt but with the help of God, that this countrie will be soone reduced. And I maie assure you that when we can be quiett heer it will be great advantage to his Ma^{tys} service for I am sure no County in this Kingdome, standes better affected Soe as our only desire is that your Highness once apearing will gett some thousands hence to followe you. The worke here will be short, and the advantage greater than you can conceive, but to informe you more particularly the bearer hereof will relate to you at better leasure. I beseech you S^r give creditt to him for he understandes the Countrie right, and will represent unto you nothing but the truthe. It will be a greate favour to me if you please to take notice of him, as one that hath done faithfully great service heer

I beseech God prosper you, & guide you heer, it will be the greatest comfort that can come unto

Your Highness
Most humble and faithfull Servant
DERBY.*

[No. 13.]

May it please your Highnesse

The returne of my Lo Biron is with that consideration taken to what concernes your comonwealth, as for

* See Introduction, p. xxi. et seq.

the matter of the result & the persons called to councell (among whom hee was a principall adviser) about it, & the whole state of the Kings affaires, as I suppose the satisfaction to your reason in the opinions are inclined to, is so probable, as by it in part you may perceive, as also from other reasons, that no Oxford motion if rightly represented (I know not what particular letters might carrie, or from whom they might be sent) could mouve any cause of Jealousie of a dessigne here ether to forestall your judgement or prelimett your comand. I have bine present at most of the consultations (till yesterday some occasions made mee absent, & of that daies work my Lo^d Biron will give the best account) & in all what I could ever discerne the proceeding hath bine to propound only by way of question all thinges of moment which were to be attended to bee acted by you or within your command, to receive an absolute resolution according to your judgement and likeing; what may have appeared more positive, as the settinge downe the Kinges condition here; the urgency as was then thought in time, and the nature of the thing itselfe, to which perhaps being absent you could not therefore so well speake to make that at first bee ventured on before it was possible to aske your opinion of it, but the inferences upon it in relation to you were never so forward to conclude beyond wishes & the ingenuitie of not disguising so much as was, is some proofe faire dealing was meant where plainesse was used. I think I could not have mist myselfe so much, if other had bine to bee seene, or where the Kinges service, and my ancient respect to Prince Rupert (which time workes no so earthy effects upon as to decay) call for my observation, that my senses could be deceived, or I not attentive. The most that was treated was when W. Legge was here, & in his companie (who certainlie is a safe man to consult with in your interests) & the furthest discourse, which was but discourse nether was but in a case of such a necessitie as imported more than Oxford, whether prevention of force were not more eligible than reparations in hopes of growing advantages, considering along the whole conjuncture of affaires, & then if anything of consequence were to be done, the fate of all the Kinges good fortune must bring Prince Rupert to have a part in it, & upon those premises the conclusion will beare his contentment which I shall ever wish as a great meanes before hand to procure those successes will cause it, and in this think I expresse myselfe

Your Highnesse
Most humble most obedient Servant

Oxford   J. RICHMOND & LENOX*
April 21
  at night

[No. 14.]

May it pleas your Highness

    With all the expedistion possibly I coulde I have sent thees Dragoneers after you I besitch God send Y^r Highness better sucses then I had with them, for both thay and my horsmen did most shaamfully loos the bravest designe at Henley that ever was undertaken sins my cooming to this Armey, and lost it not but gave the victory away when they had allready possession of all that thay went for, and with it I lost as brave an offiser as I must ever hope to comand in this Kingdom. May it pleas Y^r Highnes I am soe extreamly dejected at this busines that I doe wish with all my harte that eather I

---

   * James Stuart, Duke of Richmond and Lenox, K.G., Lord Steward of the Household. See Introduction, p. xxxvii.

had sum German souldiers to commaund, or that I coulde infuse sum German corradge into them, for Y^r English Commen souldiers are so poore and base that I could never have a greater afliction light uppon me than to bee put to command any of them I besitch y^r highnes to present my humble services unto Lift^{et} Generall Willmot, I am loth to repeat my disasters too often or els I would have written also unto him, whom I know will suffer in his thought with me

    Your Highnes most humble
      and most faithfuil servant,
         A. ASTON.*

Reading
 22 Janr.

The ennemy weare but 600 in Henley but yesterday theer came in a 1000 foot mor they have also therein 7 troops of hors and 8 pces of cannon.

[No. 15.]

Honored Syr

 As by my laste I gave you an accounte of my releeving [Relfall] castle soe by these I must acquainte you with the ill newes of its being treacherously solde by him I lefte to commande there who being a soldier sent to me by my Lo. Generall and carrying himselfe very well at that tyme the Prince tooke the close I thought might have been trusted but it moste unhappily proves othereways for after a nights fight having killed and hurte forty men felle to treat and concluded to deliver it up for a certaine some of money which treachery is noe small trouble to

---

 * Sir Arthur Aston, Colonel-General of the Dragoons in the Royal army, 1642.

mee. Syr I assure you my wante of armes makes the service I ought to doe the King very difficulte the Rebells lying upon mee one every side and within walls that I canne attempt nothing against them but when they come out to mee which they doe not but upon advantag of my absense and that hath made Ashley often troubled with them I having not lane there this monthe the force of Graye and Gell met them the other night (I being in this Cownty) tooke some men and horse in the town and soe returnede. As I am writing I receave a letter from His Majestie commanding mee to observe the motions of the Rebells and if they marche that way to followe them and joine with Lo^r. Cayrell as there shall be ocasion in all which particulers I shall be very obedient and will suddenly send into Lancashire to be informed from thence and give daily advertisements to Prince Rupert and yourself. Yet they lie in their garrisons nor canne I learne they intende to shewe only Gray is marchte with some troopes but whether to Essex or [Enicd] I am not certaine You shall hear daly from me that am

                Your affectionate friend & servant

Tutburry Castle   F. HASTINGS.*

   Sonday one in the
        afternoon

Addressed. For his Maiestie special service
To the Right Hono^{ble} Syr Edward Nicholas Knight
    Principal Secretary of State at Oxford

Haste, haste   Present this

Poste haste   F. HASTINGS.

   * Ferdinando, eldest son of Henry, 5th Earl of Huntingdon; summoned to Parliament as Baron Hastings, Nov. 3, 1640; and succeeded to the earldom, Nov. 14, 1643, and this letter must consequently have been written before that date.

[No. 16.]

May it please y^r Highns

I have received too comandes from his Ma^{tye} one by the hande of Mr. Secretary Niclas, the other ye Lo Digbyes, the latter confines mee by a narrow compass: he comandes mee to take but a 1,000 foot and a 160 horse and noe more, and yeat expects I should advance neare Gloster wheare the Rebells are 1,700 foot & Horse, Besydes I understande y^t the Horse wch came out of Ireland that were assined me are otherwayes disposed of, I beseach y^{ou} S^r lett mee have a convenient power to doe it, and a meanes for theire subsistance, or lett me begeinn wheare I may with best safety wch is in ye welch syde, my Lo Herbert hath brought a commission for Coll Slaughter to be s^{r}jent major Generall of the horse & my Lo Digbye wrights it is thought fitteing that Sr Francis Hawlye should have the comand of the Horse under mee (how to behave myself in this I know not,) nor do I understande in what condition I myself am in. My Lo Herbert is Generall, and yeat all [   ] are directed to mee, wch is not very pleasinge to his Excellency

S^r I humbly beg y^r Highn^s: pardon this troble ye receive from

S^r

Y^r Highn^s most humble Servant
WILL VAVASUR.*

* Sir William Vavasour, Clarendon states, "commanded all the forces in South Wales (the Lord Herbert having been persuaded so far to comply with the indisposition of that people as to decline that command, or at least for a time to dissemble it), as orders were despatched to him to draw all his forces to the forest side of the town" (Gloucester). Later on, however, he states, "his," the king's, "army would receive a very great addition by a body of three thousand men, which was commanded by Vavasour on the Welch side to block up Gloucester from annoying the country." Probably therefore the suggestion made by Sir William Vavasour in this letter was attended to.

[No. 17.]

May it please your Highnesse
  September 18 at one in the morning
    [1643]

I have lett the King see what you writt who approuves of all in it, and will accordingly performe his part, only desires to have certaine knowledge when Essex mouved or shall mouve from Creklade, that if his Maj^{ties} armie can come time enough (which he will ghesse at by the answer) hee will take up his quarter this night at, or about Wantage, so to reach Newberry as you propose, but if that cannot bee hee is loath to wearie the foote after so great a march as they have had, which you know inferrs that manie are behind; Last night my Ld Digby writt to your Highnesse by the Kings order upon the receipt of yours from Stamford,* to which I can adde what is only knowne since that beside Vavisor & some other forces Woodhouse will I am confident come to-day to the King (with Prince of Wales regement called 700) Hee lay last night at a place called Warmington & I then sent one who came from him imediately to give him order to march presently hither to the King, which I suppose may be soone enough to keepe pace with the motions of our armie, which depends much as the advertizements from you will give information. The King will acquaint my Ld Generall with what your Highnesse now receives from your most humble Servant

J. R. & L.

* This letter is printed in "Rupert and the Cavaliers," vol. ii. p. 290, and refers, together with the letter now published, to the evolutions immediately preceding the battle fought at Newbury, after the siege of Gloucester had been abandoned.

[No. 18.]

May it please your Highnesse

That which concernes dispatch or answer to business you will constantly receive from Mr. Secr Nicholas, who in that writes for the whole companie, & my particular care is not wanting in that, but what is more attentivelie my studdy, is what may have any referrence to yourselfe and therfore upon the receipt of yours last night, perceiveing, your Highn^s, from a hint taken of a letter from L^d D* was in doubt that at Oxford there might bee wrong judgements made of you and of businesse in your quarters, I made it my dilligence to cleare with the King (who answers the same for the Queene) which was easie; so as you may bee satisfied, no scruple at all ether is, or was, of your actions, this I say the lesse in, because you will bee assured of the same by my Ld Jermyn, considering the jealousie might have growne from some doubtful expressions in that letter you mention, I spoke with the partie how it was understood from his hand who seemed much grieved at it, assuring hee write only the advice of such intelligence as was brought hether, & for information, to make use of as you could best judge how upon the place. Yesterday one brought me your Comission to peruse, but it was under the great seale, so as if not so perfect as were requisite amendments could not bee made without beginning all againe, but I did not find that necessitie, for I looked it over & I thinke it is carefully drawne. Wee heare my Ld Hopton† is Marcht. Ld Goring‡ is well arrived in Holland & by this is to-

* Lord Digby.

† Sir Ralph Hopton was created Lord Hopton in Aug. 1643. On 3rd Nov. Nicholas wrote to Prince Rupert that Lord Hopton had marched to relieve Winchester.

‡ Lord Goring, sent as Ambassador to Paris in the autumn of 1643.

wards goeing on his journey & now the King is hie to church which cutts of this

    Your Highnesse
      Most humble Servant
9ber   I. RICHMOND & LENOX.
 (November 1643).

[No. 19.]

May it please your Highnesse

 I have not before this, since yours of the 14th presumed to troubled to you because the importance of the Action you were about was (and as by the successe to your great glorie, joy of your friends and happinesse of all) & is now knowne so considerable, as it would have bine great indiscretion in that time to have given any occasion to lead away any thought from what did so much require them, but this being a time of gladnesse, as the other was of care, in you for the publicke, & in all for you: give mee leave to dilate now upon my particular joyes, & to retire them so farre from the present Jubile all men are in at your last great victorie,* as to beginne with that which, before this Jubile, was one to mee, the honor & contentment I latelie received from you, which if value can make precious, & an intent affection doe anything to show an acknowledgement, will not bee lost upon mee. Your comand to pray for you at a time was then to come shall bee as before my Generall rule what is to bee done, look into all future times & this upon which you directed it be now passt I must joine it to the rest, that is so & the same way to, of praise, still greater cause of addition growing. So the division of

   * The storming of Newark.

present thoughts and wishes to come hath this subject, to observe what is due to you & for you. This is the generall I hope I shall not faile on my part of the practise

Your Highnesse
Most humble most obedient Servant
J. RICHMOND & LENOX.

Oxford March 25
 at night

[No. 20.]

May Itt please your Highnes

 You are welcoume S^r so manaye severall wayes, as itt is beyonde my Arethmetick to number, butt this I knowe you are the redemer of the North & the savior of the Crowne. Your name S^r hath terefide thre greate Generalls & theye flye before itt. Itt seemes theyer designe is nott to meet your Highnes for I beleve theye have gott a river betweene you and them butt they are so newlye gone as ther is [no] sertentie att all of them or their Intentions, neyther Can I resolve any thinge since I am made of nothing butt thankfulness & obedience to your Highnes comandes

Your Hignes most obligde
&
Most obedient Servant
W. NEWCASTLE.*

Yorke
 July the first
  1644

---

* William Cavendish, Marquis of Newcastle, Lieutenant-General of the Royal armies north and south of Trent. See p. xlix.

[No. 21.]

Maie it please your Highnesse

In all places where I come, its my misfortune to meete wth extreame trouble. The Gaurisons not able to bee maintayned by the Contributions belonginge to them, & yet the horse not so considerable in number as I wish: And they unwillinge to goe out upon the Enemy (especially such as goe under the name of Reformadoes) they shoote not sufficient to maintayne the Garrisons against a Scidge, the provisions therein much wasted & the making of Powder & Match in all places at a Stand (wch wth all possible speed I am pressinge to set forward) The Souldiers (cheifly the Governors) discontented at the Comissioners, & the Country people much exasperated against the pressures of the Souldiers: so that they have been ready to rise against the Guarisons, but as yet are quieted. I have mett in this place wth an exceedinge great trouble the comanders & souldiers in the Close at Litchfield havinge shut out my Lo Loughborough, all or most of the Officers articuled against him to the Kinge: Yet I finde their Complaints not so much againste his Lo{p} himselfe as some learned Reformadoes that appertayne to him, & the most of these who complaine of him confessinge Courtesyes received from his Lo{p} However I finde they have wth joynet consent taken an Oath or Protestation of fidelity to the Kinge, & another to runne all one waye in defence of what they have donn To reconcile this business, I desired my Lo Loughborough's coming hither, & wrought so farr with the Officers as they all were ready to give him satisfaction, acknowledg their Errour & crave his pardon in publique. But of this his Lo{p} would not accept; but would have a Counsell of Warre called wch will aske

tyme; I cannot stay. And, in the mean tyme, if I
should comit any of them (as in such a case ought to bee)
All the officers are so linked togeather, & all the Souldiers
have such dependence on them, not having half men
enough to put in & remove them; a greate Inconvenience
certainly would ensue to the prejudice of his Ma^s Service,
by the probable apprehension of their Errours. So in
this nature I have left the place, under the comand of
Sr Thomas Tyldesley & Colonell Henry Bagot & am
going to Tutbury & after to Bridgnorth, whence I received
lres from the Comisioners there of the daunger by
practises of the Enemy upon that place, & some discon-
tents agaiest Sr Lewis Kirke, now gonn for Oxford. Thus
having given y Highnesse a breif accompt of the state
of thinges heere, I humbly take leave & rest

  S^r

   Y^r Highnesses most humble Servant

      JACOB ASTELEY.*

Litchfield 12 Jan 1645.

[No. 22.]

Illustrious Prince

  Altho the multiteude of Y^r Highnes more wyghtie
affairs be argument sufficient to inhibitt my importenning
Y^r Hg^s with my wrytting yet the multiteud of grieffs I
suffer by some bad information I understand Y^r Highnes
have receaved of me, since my parting w^h Y^r Hg^s inforces
me to present to Y^r Highnes vew what I heave heard,
to witt, that Y^r Hg after I was gon to Skearsbrough

 * Sir Jacob Astley, Major-General of the Foot in the Royal army,
1642, was created Baron Astley of Reading, Nov. 4, 1644. He was
now Field-Marshal-General. See Introduction, p. xxvi.

should heave sent to steay me and to recall me bak and that by reson of som tratourous act Y^r Highnes had to leay to my cheardge, as for the [first] which was steaying of me If yor Hg^s at my teaking my leave from you had leavyd Yo^r least commands or desyrs upon me, they should heave been obeyed, and if Yo^r Hygnes heave anything to leay to my chearge, I can but answyr Yo^r Hig^{nes} as I have wryttin to His sacred Matie wch was that I wold apeir when and wher His sacred Matie wold command me eather to cleir myselfe or suffer for my offence. The same I offer to Y^r Hyghnes for I reather suffer any thing in the world then leive innocentlie in Y^r Highnes Malgreace, for I dear plead my tho^{ts} innocent from ay prejudiciall thing to my measter his searvice or hurtfull to Yo^r princelie feamalie to my knowledg and I dout not bot yor Hy^s can bear me witnes in a peart. I in all hemilitie creav yor Hyghnes pardonn for my bouldnes and begg Y^r Hygnes gratious answer w^h yor spidiest convenience to him who shall ever remeayn

    Yo^r Hyghnes
      trowlie devoyted Servant

Hamburrie Y^e   ETHYN.*

 23 of January 1645

Yo^r Hyghnes will excuse the informalitie of this letter my sicknes is the cause of it for I heave beine above 4 months sick

---

[No. 23.]

May it please Y^r Highness

  When I have ask't your pardon for this presumption and trouble wth your leave I shall haste to the

* Sir James King, Knt., of Barracht, Lieutenant-General under the Marquis of Newcastle in the North, created Lord Ethyn, in Scotland, March 28, 1643.

occasion of this letter; Your old and faithfull Servant Captn Jo: Reichardson is heere in Y^e King's service as diligent as his usual custome and inclination wth his old troope and hartes; If it please your Highness it was Y^e Kings command to mee hee should heer joyne wth us butt people dispos'd to make groundless carrells beginn Y^e symptomes of a murmure; Y^r Knowledge of this may prepare you against those litle engines of discontent; I am confident you understande mee in this particular; and by this lighte you shall bee unprinced if you beleeve mee nott.

S^r

Y^e most humble

Off Y^r Servants

J. O. GRANDISON.

Harrington Feb.^{r} Y^e 7
    1645

[No. 24.]

May it please Yr Highness

I finde now there is little hope that my Lord of Loughborough will satisfy Yr Highness expectation, and therefore upon the first oportunity I shall attempt to passe for Oxford, I cannot by any means get the fifty pounds which I received here returned, but if any will pay it at Oxford he shall have it certainly upon your Highness's signification thereof repayed him here. The Lo Ashtely is returned and after the reliefe of Maxfield, pursued the Rebells and tooke two pieces of Ordnance, some of them got into a church and maintained the Steeple untill they were fired out. here is not any of the 4000 men which were undertaken at Oxford to [be] recuited, yet levyd, nor cannot be considered possible by any rationall men, the Enemy is active in every place, but here wee live as if possest with a lethargy. I shall ever pray for Yr Highness happiness remaining

   Yr H^s
    Most obedient Servant,
      RALPH GOODWIN.*

Worcester
  Feby 7 1645

[No. 25.]

S^r

By this inclosed you perceive the distresses of the North and now the choice is whether you will desert Y^r Countrie now gained & possest or serve against a fresh enemie I pray resolve speedily of it; and make all the haste hither you may it is very fitt the Prince be acquainted with it for if S^r Th. Fairfax joyne with the Rebells all these forces in these pts and those in Darbyshire must joyne and follow them Sir a counsell of warr must necessarily be called, & the prince acquainted with it.

    Your most faithfull Servant
28 March   S. TUKE.†
  Lincoln
   Addressed
  These for the honorable Mr. Porter Major Generall at Newark

---

* Probably Ralph Goodwin, M.P. for Ludlow, 1640.
† Samuel Tuke, Colonel in the Royal army; created a Baronet, March 31, 1664.

[No. 26.]

May it please Y Highness

Just as I was coming to my quarters about 9 a clock I had intelligence by a couple of prissoners taken by the quarter maister of Worcester Collonell Sandes that puphery iss quartered att Camden this night 5 troopes of [and] 2 of Dragoones, and that this morning he came from Warwyck. As yett I understand nothing to the contrary that he is not ther: to all the quarters round a bout I gave notice. Sands & Collonell Westons regiments are drawn between him and Warwyck I am now going towards him on this siyd, by brak of day iff they answer our resolution: I hope wee shall make him pay for our losse att his house of this I thought fitt to aquaint Yr highness. Iff any orders cam^d it should not find here

Yr highness's most humble Servant

DANIELL O'NEILLE.*

Broadway.

[No. 27.]

Charles R

Whereas Our Right Deare & entirely beloved Nepheu Prince Rupert did at a Councill of warr held by us at Newarke the 18th of this instant October there being then present Our Right trusty & Right well beloved Cosen & Councillor Mountague Erle of Lyndsey Lord Great Chamberlayne of England Our Right trusty & Right well beloved Cosen Richard Erle of Corke, Our

* Lieutenant-Colonel of Prince Rupert's Regiment of Horse; afterwards Groom of the Bedchamber to the King. See Introduction, p. lv. Several characteristic letters of O'Neille will be found in Carte's "Collection of Original Letters and Papers concerning England," from 1641 to 1660.

Right trusty & well beloved Jacob Lord Asteley Field Marshall Generall of Our Army John Lord Bellasis Captaine Generall of Our Horse Guards, & Charles Lord Gerrard Lieutenant Generall of all Our Horse Forces, Our trusty & well beloved Sr Richard Willis Knight & Baronett Governor of Newarke, & John Ashburnham Esq Our Treasurer at warr, desire to cleere himselfe for the rendering of the City & Garrison of Bristoll with the Castle & Forces thereof, & thereupon produced a narrative of the matter of fact during the said siedge with the Articles for the rendering of those places, which being accordingly read & considered Wee were then pleased to say that Wee did not believe Our said Nepheu to be guilty of any the least want of courage or fidelity to us in the doing thereof but withall we believed that he might have kept the Castle & Fort a longer tyme Wee having absolutely resolved speedily to have drawen together all the Forces we possibly could & to have hazarded Our Own Person for his relief, Our Design being so layed as that in probability it would have succeeded. To which Our said Right Deare Nepheu answered that what ever hee did therein was by the advice of the Councell of warr of that Garrison, & that he could not in his Judgment possibly expect such reliefe besides hee alleadged that hee had not received from Us any intimation thereof but said that if hee had he would have mayneteyned those places to the last man though the tender reguard he had to the preservation of so many Officers & Souldiers was the chiefe reason that induced him to capitulate for the whole they having so long & faithfully served Us All which our said Right Deare Nepheu humbly submitted to our Judgment

Upon which at a Second hearing before Ourselfe this 21st day of October the Lords & others above named being then likewise present & upon a serious consideration of the whole matter wee were then pleased to declare that Wee were fully satisfyed that Our said Right Deare Nepheu Prince Rupert is not guilty of any the least want of courage or fidelity to Us or Our service in that Action, & Wee then gave leave to the Lords & other abov specified to declare their oppenions in that poynt.

Who upon Our leave & a full consideration of the narrative formerly delivered did unanimously concurre with us, declaring likewise that Our said Right Deare Nepheu is not guilty of any the least want of courage or fidelity to Us or Our service in that Action. Given under Our Signe Manuall at Our Court at Newark this 21 October 1645

By his Mat[ies] Command

EDW WALKER.*

[No. 28.]

May it please Y[r] Highnesse

This nyght I was wth the King whoe expresses greate kindnesse to you, but beleevs Y[r] partinge wth him was soe much the contrary as Y[r] Hignesse cannot think it but a finill. How truly Sir his Majestye conceaving it soe in my oppinion tis fftt you should make sume hansume applycation, for this reason, because my Lord Duke and others here are much Y[r] servants, And all that are soe wish yre returne to Courte, though it be but to part frendlye but I think it necessary you prepar the waye first by letters to the King. S[r] I have no designs in this but Y[r] servyce, and if you understand me rightlye

* Sir Edward Walker, Knt., Secretary to the Council of War; afterwards Garter King-at-Arms, and Clerk of the Council.

that will prevayle soe much as you will consyder what I saye, before you resolve the contrarye, I knowe there be sume are your enemys but they are such as may barcke, but I am confident are not able to fytt ag^t you, appeare therefore S^r I beseech you Doe not contrybute to the satysfaction of yr foes and ruyne of yr frends by neglectinge any things wth in yr power to make peace with fortune. If after all yr attempts to be rightlye understood you shall fayle of that, yet you cannot waynt honor for that action, tis Y^r Uncle you shall submit to And a Kinge not in a condition he mery^t What others may saye I know not but really S^r may I speak my opinyon as a person that values you above all the world besydes. I am confident you know how faithfully my harte is to your Highnes And how much I am

   Your Highnesses most obedient humble
      Servant

Oxford this Thursday
night 3 o'Clock.

      [No date or signature.]

[No. 29.]

May it please your Highnesse

  This morninge I presented your letter to the Lords who have resolved to grant your desires in it and have sent it downe to the house of Commons for their agreement with them and upon Monday it will be consented to there [

   ] make the greatest haste I can, the [

     ] and shall give you further intelligence of my proceedings as there shall be occasion, in the meane time S^r I thought it my duty to acquaint you with thus much, and that I am faithfully

    Your Highnesse
        Most obedient Servant
                HEN OSBORNE.*

London Novemb
    the 1 1645

[No. 30.]

May it please your Highness

    The King hath commanded me to signify to yor highness that Coll Will. Leg hath faithfully delived to his Ma^{ty} all he had in command from yor to wch his Ma^{ty} hath taken only some little excepsons, wch the Collonell hath only from the King to acquaint yor highnes wth all by word to whom his Ma^{ty} desires yor to give cred this being all I have in command at p^{r}sent to deliver to yor hignes from his Mat^y I humbly rest

    S^r
        Yo^r highnes
            Most humble Servant
                EDW NICHOLAS.†

Oxon 7 Decr 1645
(addressed)
    ffor his Highnes
        Prince Rupert att
            Woodstock-these

---

* See Introduction, p. lxxix.   † Secretary of State.

[No. 31.]

To his Excellencie Sr Thomas Firefax generall of the Parliamen Forces.

The humble peticon of the Inhibants of the Prsh of Westbury in the County of Wilts

Sheweth

That yor poore peticone^s are willing to undergoe theire pporconable tax of the generall burthen of this Kingdom according to yor Excellencies declaracons and the ordinances of parliament, pvided that wee may be tyed to no other inconvenience than yor Excellencies declaracons & the ordinances of parliam^t doe divulge   And that yor peticoners may be at a certainty to know the worst of o^r sufferings wch we shall cheerefully undergoe for the furtherance of the publique goode in relacion to the parliam^t and armie   And whereas the parliam^t and yor Excellencie in goodnesse have afforded us very goode orders and declarons the benefits whereof wee want videlt that if the country shall pay the 60000^l p mensem they shall be freed from free quarters   Whereof six monethes demandes we have already payde and the other three monethes now questioned wee are ready to pay and yet are constantly burthened wth free quartering and that wch hath next relacon to free quarter as may appeare by o^r accompte of the charge wch the sayde towne and pish have beene at wch amounts to above the pporcon of o^r rate for the 60000^l p mensem already the continuance of wch y^r poore peticoners are not able to undergoe   And whereas the rumo^r of the souldiers paying for theire quarters may appeare to the world to be somthing yet wee find it in effect nothing or wthin one degree of free quarter as shall appeare to yor Excellencie and the parliam^t videlt that a Troope of

Dragoones of one hundred besides Officers under the commaund of captain Barrington, pᵣtending yoʳ Excellencies order, have quartered upon us thirty dayes already and those who refuse to quarter them are constraynᵈ to pay 3ˢ a day for horse and man, pʳtending that they will discharge theire quarters when they receive their pay wᶜʰ pay being by them received yoʳ peticoners canne make it appeare that they received not above the fifth pte of what the charge of quartering amounts unto. So that yoʳ peticonʳˢ are like to undergoe the burthen of free quarters and pay theire rates to boote unless the parliamᵗ and yoʳ Excellencie be pleased to consider the distressed estate of this country.

Yoʳ peticonʳˢ having delivered the grievances of this psh doe humbly desire yoʳ Excellencie to consider of the destressed estate wee are now in being the least and poorest hundred in the county as will appeare to yoʳ Excellencie upon further examinacon And doe farther desier that yoᵘ will be pleased to give us a positive order under yoʳ hand and seale what yoʳ peticoners shall allow the souldiers upon a march or upon a settled quarter And in regard we have formerly suffered so farre beyond other places we humbly desire that we may be freed from that settled quarter both for the tyme pʳsent and future, unlesse it bee uppon a march for a night or two, that so we may avoyde the commaund of the soulders or to be at theire disposure and yoʳ peticonʳˢ shall as in duty bound ever pray for yoʳ Excellencie

February this last
   1647.

                THOMAS HANCOCKE, Mayor.

Here follow twelve other signatures.

A Rate made for the maintaynance of Sr Thos Firfix Armie.

Bratton	25
Westbury	12 & halfe
Chantrey	12 & halfe
Borough	4 & halfe
Heywood	12 & halfe
Brooke	18 & quarter
Ligh	5 & halfe
Bayly in ligh	9 & halfe
Lambridge Prior	3
Shortsbrett	3 & quarter
Chapmanslade	3 & quarter
Henby	12 & quarter
Dilton	5 & halfe
Bayley in H Lawbridge	3 & halfe

The Names of the 3 soulders that quartere at the Bell{e}.

William Birein
John Gilbert
William Broughton.

[No. 32.]

According as by order we weare required: we have considered; & cannot find of what tything ye vicarige of Westbury is: for we never find yt it was rated formerly by any tything as a member thereof. Also we have considered of its value: and doo conceave yt it is worth about £60 0s. 0d. p. anum in ye full But ye burdens of cures & thenthes discharged it is worth about £25 0s. 0d. p annum wich being an inconsiderable sum for yᵉ maintenance of yᵉ vicar and his familie therfor the parish hath not formerly nor ded we now think him fitt to be rated to any tax but are content to exempt him and to beare yᵉ proportion allotted to yᵉ Tythings wʰthout him nether have we rated the Chantery tything above its due valew wʰthout the addition of yᵉ vicarige to it

the Dues of the vicarige as folloeth

£	s.	d.	
45	0	0	the woll
12	0	0	the Compoˢ for mills &c.
3	0	0	for other paltry dues
60	0	0	

Of this he Doth paye as folloeth

£	s.	d.	
20	0	0	a year to Bratton
10	0	0	a yeare to Dolton
4	10	0	tenthes besids charges for the gathering of it therfor we will intret you to considder what [ ] will be left to maintain a mennester if he most paye taxses.

Signed by John Edwards & Thomas Marchaunt Constables and Eight Assessors

---

[No. 33.]

Sir

Although not allowed by this Committee yet it hath pleased the Comittee of Lords & Commons upon a due and serious examination, to confirme the deede showed by Mr. Seymour and in persuance to that, have granted an order to the Committee of Wilts for taking off the sequestration. I sent this bearer as well wth the Order it selfe as also wth all the proceedings hoping he should have met the Comittee for Wilts at Malberow but meeting only Mr Martyn there he advised this bearer to repayre to you and Mr Selfe to whom I have given directions to attend on you both desyring you get your hand likewise. So I rest

   Your very loving ffriend & Servant
         ANW SEYMOUR.

Salisbury
 July 16, 1647

[No. 34.]

         Paris Decem 18

My dearest Cousin

 If I had not thought you would have bene heare before this time, I would have written offtener and fuller to you: The truth is I do only deferr the setting downe the time of my goeing from hence and the resolving wch way to goe, till I speake with you, you know what I am promised to receave from the French Court for my journey, in the meane time I am sure I am not only without money, but have bene compelled to borrow all that I have spent neere these 3 months so that you will easily judge how soone three thousand and six hundred pistols will be gone, and yett I must expect no more from hence, but depend upon what you shall bring me, for my shipp, gunnes, and my share of the prize. I longe to have you here, and am interely

   dearest Cousin
    Your most affectionate Cousin
        CHARLES R.

For my dearest Cousin
  Prince Rupert

No. 35.

My very good Lord

I looke upon his Highness Prince Rupert as a person who besides his greate worth and quality I doe honor and regarde as one in whome wee doe place our greatest hopes of being the chiefe instrument of the Kinges restablishment, and because I am wholly unknowne unto him I humbly pray Y^r Lo^p who have as I am persuaded a principal interest in his Highnes to lett him know what you doe conceive of mee both in respect of the little experience I have acquird in the world, and my particular devotion to his service of which if his Highnes will please for to make a triall & take mee into his care and owne me procuring mee from his Mas^y a present reliefe and meanes to subsist either in the place I am in or where I shall bee judgd more usfull for the publick service I will have my whole dependency on his Highnes & apply my selfe so entirely unto him as hee shall have no cause to complaine of this office which I pray your Lo^p to performe unto him for

Your Lo^p

Most humble Servant

DE VIC*

I pray y^r Lo^p to procure mee a speedie answere for I am in a condition that will admit of noe delay In extreme want as you may see by this letter

Brux 7 June 1653

* Sir Henry De Vic, of Guernsey, Envoy-Resident at Brussels for nearly twenty years; created a Baronet, Sept. 3, 1649; afterwards Chancellor of the Order of the Garter.

[No. 36.]

Collogne 6 Feb^r St No 165$\frac{5}{8}$

May it please y^r Highnes

Understanding by Mr. Beynl of Ffrancfort that y^r Highnes was expected shortly in these partes I would not fayle to present my humble duty and service to you with such advertisements as I have latest had from Engl^d. This being now my 5th letter sent yo^u since y^r Hignes commanded me to correspond wth you which I hope are come to your hands, though I have not heard as yet whether y^r Highnes hath received any of them The Princess Royal was expected round to Paris Tuesday last being att Peronne friday was senight where the Duke of Yorke and my Lo Gerrard met her R.H. having attended there for her some dayes before. I have herein sent yr High^s an extract of such advertisem^{ts} as I have had last from Engl^d being the most certayne that wee have receaved from that miserable kingdom. Dr Fraissar attended the Princess Roy^{al} to Paris and how long he intends to remayne there is not certayne. I heard from Holl^d that Cromwell being by Newport ye D. ambdor in Engl^d pressed to acquaint the States wth ye severall Articles between him and France, refuses it, where at the States are much unsatisfyed with Cromwell. Its alsoe written from Holl^d that Newport having lately spoken wth Cromwell concerning the king of Swedens proceedings against the Pr^n Elec^r of Brandenburg, that Cromwell answered him, that albeit he wished well to Sweden whilst he prosecuted warre in Poland yet now that he findes he hath turned his armes against the Protestant Princes & Townes he will have noe more to doe wth that king; But though possibly this may be said by him to

Newport (of whose person & of whose Masters Cromwell hath noe esteeme att all) Yet I am confident it hath been meerely to cajole them, for its most certayne but Cromw^{ll} is extraordinarily carefull & is very intimate with the Sweedishe Ambdor now in Engl^d & in like manner the K. of Sweden with his (one Rolt) Cromwells envoye now in their Army with him with exceeding great kindness and respect; soe as its evident there is still a very close intelligence betweene the K. of Sweden and Cromwell. By lres from fraunce its advertized that the Articles of Peace & agreement betweene that Crowne and Crom^{ll}, are by a particular clause & condition to be signed w^{thin} a limitted tyme as well by the Princes of the bloud in france as by the ff^r King, or else to be invallid; and some are of opinion that this hath bene one principall means of the D. of Orleans being called to the ff^r Court where he is dayly expected; but there is noe speech of his daughter Mademoiselles peace being yet made. We heard that the Hollan^{drs} have 48 sayl of men of warre, which will be ready to sett sayle for the Baltick Seas as soone as the season will permitt: We heerd that the Erle of Glenearne and other Scot^{ch} Ld^s who made their Peace lately with Monke, upon their leaving the L G^{ll} Middleton are lately upon new frends and therefore imprisoned by Monke   The letters brought by this dayes post from Bruxelles as well from his Maj^{ty} resident there as from many others assure us that orders are now come from Madrid to ye King of Spains [Minister] in Flanders to take effectual orders to psecute the warre against Cromwell and his fellow Rebells in England and to that end to prokure lres of mark against the Englishe, wherin the adm^{ty} in Flanders are att present very busy and sollicitous : Svrall letters from Spayne also now advertyse that * * * is in his warre ag^t Crom^{ll} resolved to espouse his maj^tes [my masters] quarrell, whereof I will expect shortly to see good effects, for that we heare the Comittee in Flanders sitt now dayly to consult of all means to oppose and divert Cromwells designs and enterprizes; & will expect shortly to have an order or direcson from ye Arch Duke & his Councell, that all the K of Spaynes Portes in Flanders and [else where] shall be free and secure: for any English or others that will repayre into them to serve against Cromwell & the Rebells in Engl^d. The Princesse Royall was expected to be att Paris Tuesday last and the ff^r King & the Queene his mother intended to meete her Roy^l High^s a league out of Paris to bring her into that Citty. The D. of Modena is sayd to be returned from * * * towards July All lres by this post from England confirme the news Cromw^ll being in great fryghte att present, & of the change of his gards, having now every nyght 60 soldiers that gard him where he lodges If I understand that this comes safe to y^r Highnes, I shall contynue to send you such occurences as we have here, in obedience to the comand receaved from you by

  Your Highn^s
    Most humble and most obedient Servant
      EDW NICHOLAS.

LETTERS FROM

LORD PERCY

TO THE

KING & PRINCE RUPERT.

[NOTE.]

THE writer of the following letters was Henry Percy, brother to the Earl of Northumberland. He was created Lord Percy in 1643 at the instance of the Queen.

Percy was one of those who were active in endeavouring to save the life of Strafford, and in his efforts for that end was the means of winning Hyde over to the Royal cause. In Lord Clarendon's biography (p. 42, edit. 1759) it is stated that Percy introduced him to the King after a conversation of which no other record is remaining. Involved in the "Army Plot" and wounded by the country people in Sussex, he with difficulty escaped to his brother's residence in London. "The Earl," says Clarendon, " being in great trouble, had to send him away beyond the seas after his wound was cured, advised with a friend then in power, and who innocently enough brought Mr. Pym into the council, who over-witted them both by frankly consenting that Mr. Percy should escape into France, upon condition that the Earl first drew from him such a letter as might by the party be applied as evidence of the reality of the plot."*

Percy was Master-General of the Ordnance during the period over which these letters extend, and was deprived of that office by the King, who conferred it on Lord Hopton in the autumn of 1644.

* Clarendon, vol. i. p. 744.

Clarendon evidently was no friend of Percy, and on the occasion of his dismissal thus speaks of him : " Yet even his removal added to the ill-humour of the army, too much disposed to discontent, and censuring all that was done; for though he was generally unloved, as a proud and supercilious person, yet he had always three or four persons of good credit and reputation who were esteemed by him, with whom he lived very well, which, in the general scarcity of that time, drew many votaries to him, who bore very ill the want of his table, and so were not without some inclination to murmur even of his behalf."*

Lord Percy, if we may judge from the letters of Arthur Trevor to Prince Rupert, was no favourite with the former. Writing from Oxford on 22 Feb., 1644, to the Prince, Trevor says : " My Lord Percy is still in the briars, and I believe will not get out without scratches ; but if they prove no more, they will be physical towards the spring."† This refers to some difficulties arising out of his lordship's very unsatisfactory accounts. Trevor's letters are full of complaints at the difficulty he experienced in obtaining supplies of arms and ammunition : money he declares he has no hope of. He contrasts the supplies lavished on Lord Hopton with those reluctantly doled out to the Prince, and evidently views with a strong partisan bias every pound of powder and every stand of arms despatched to the aid of the cavaliers in the West.

Several notices of Lord Percy appear from time to time in Whitelocke's Memorials, the letters of intelligence published in Thurloe's State Papers, and the correspondence between Lord Clarendon and Sir William Brown. From the first of these authorities we learn

* Clarendon, vol. iv. p. 531.
† Rupert and the Cavaliers, vol. iii. p. 377.

that in letters from the Hague, in October, 1648, it was stated "that the Lord Piercy was committed for giving the lye in the Prince's presence."* From the second, that he was in Feb., 1654, "settled in France, and hath Chastian Renard, belonging to the house of Orange."† While from the third we have an interchange of letters which may possibly bear the interpretation that in December, 1653, Clarendon was on bad terms with Lord Percy. In the letter written at that date by Sir William Brown to the then Sir Edward Hyde he says: "I did not till very lately know that the Lord Percy, now Lord Chamberlin, was come to the King, and I am likewise told he is much in your intimacy, of which, if true, I am very glad, for hee hath beene my noble friend of a date little lesse than 30 yeares old. I pray if your Hon^r think it fitt be pleased to present my humble service and congratulations to his L'pp."

To this Clarendon replied: "Though my Ld Chamberlyne and I lyve civilly togither, and I can mencon you to him, yett it is fitt you write a congratulatory letter to him, which if you think fitt, I will deliver."‡

In apparently—for the date is not given, and can only be gathered from the context—August, 1654, Col. Bampfylde thus writes of "the condition and designments of the titular King of Scots, and of those abroade, whoe are interessed in his affayres":

"His Councille are his mother, the Duke of York, Prince Rupert, the duke of Buckingham, the marquis of Ormonde, the earle of Rochester, the lords Percye, Jermin, Inchequin, Taff lately made, and Sir Edward Hide.

"The foure first, together with Jermin, are of a faction

---

* Whitelocke, p. 343.   † Thurloe, vol. ii. p. 85.
‡ Diary and Correspondence of John Evelyn, &c.. edition 1852, vol. iv. pp. 296-298.

directly opposite to Hide, and the other party who for the present intyrely governe in his councills; and theyr designes seem to be as different as theyr inclinations. Ormonde, Hide, and theyr party have, contrary to the sence of the reste, advised and prevayled with theyr king totally abandon both the party and principles of the presbiterians, and to relye intyrely upon his old episcopall party, which they perswade him comprehends the nobillity, gentry, and bulke of the kingdome of England, whoe would not rise with him in his late march into England, because he was believed to goe upon ground disagreeable both to theyr affections interests, and to the goode of the nation, and inconsistent with the ancient constitutions both of Church and State."*

* Thurloe, vol. ii. p. 510.

[No. 37.]

This relation was dated 12 at night this Monday.

S^r

Next to the waiting uppon you myselfe I am pleased with this employment being commaunded by the King to give you a relation of what hath passed at Maleborough. The delay of the Artilleryes coming up and the mistinesse of the morning made it neere 2 of the clocke before they could playe uppon the towne. It was assaulted on the Champion side and a regiment of horse sent to the forrest side to hinder there flight that way exspecting that much more then there resistance. At the first from a brest worke they had made acrosse the downe where the passage was and after from a rowe of thatcht houses they did gall our men whoe were not able to returne them any hurt by armes soe that they were necessitated to have recourse to fire which gave our men entry, whereuppon they of the towne fled but were taken in greate numbers by the regiment of horse on the other side, among which there was the principall Scotch officer one Ramsey and Francklins the towne Clarke a Prot^{nt} man and a principall incendiary of all those parts, the prisoners that were taken came to about 100 besides Diggs and his Company whoe we tooke to be frends assuring us they would not shoote and in that kept there words, they were very usefull likewise in keeping the other forces of the towne, out of my Ld Seymers house and mount that might have troubled us much. The fight lasted above 2 howres there were 20 or 30 ours hurt none of much note nor any killed, what slaughter was on the rebells side we know not, nor directly how many collors taken. After the entry of the towne the Lieut Ge^{ls} cheefe care was to stoppe the fire for the which he caused some houses to be pulled downe and drew out the troopes and Dragoneers least they should have bin lost in the night by there disorder and Pillage, which was done and they quartered all rownd about the towne, the foote only left in it, and that condition they remaine in until his Ma^{tys} pleasure be further knowne. This S^r is the substance of that relation his Ma^{ty} receaved from thence this morning and having noething else considerable at this time to accquaint you with I will begg this favor from you that I may esteemed by

        Your Hig^{nes}

           Your most humble Servant

                  HEN PERCY

Nepheu I must conjure
you as ye love me not to
hazard yourselfe nedlessly
    CR.

My Lo^d Dunsmore kisseth
your hands
    the 6th of No.   [1642.]

[No. 38.]

Sr

I promised myselfe the honor to have waited uppon you before you went away which I was prevented in yet must not give that ill fortune leave to injure me soe much as to steale you into an ill opinion of my civility or duty but preserve both by your goodnesse and this letter which is to tell you I had an intention to have waited, uppon you this journey but my Ld Spencer bringing a packett of letters from the Queene and was engaged by her to waite uppon her to the King. There letters were dated the $\frac{29}{8}$ and informe as of noe thing considerable but the Queenes preparation for her journey to which there was noe thing wanting but the comming about of some shipps that were daily expected soe that by circumstances we may guesse her landed by this time. There is one come from my Ld Newcastell this day whoe tells us my Ld Savill is prisoner at Newarke Castle and the Sheriffe of Lincolneshire did advertise the King that my Ld Newport was a prisoner to. Hastings hath receaved the enemy soe unkindly as they are retired but we heere Sr R. Hoppton is pursued hottly and being weaker then the enemy retires, so soone as Prince Maurice marched away, the enemyes forces came thither, I can hope for noe excuse for this but my being
Sr
Your most humble Servant
HEN PERCY
[Probably 21 Feb 1643]
21 Oxford

[No. 39.]

Sr

According to your commaunds I accquainted his Mat{y} with the contents of your letter which he hath consulted with my Ld Gener^l whoe is of oppinion that it will be very inconvenient for your Hig^nes to moove to Buckingham being to farre distant from Oxford which may cause some inconveniences to us heere, besides that, it appeeres not to be soe propper for that end you propose it for, there being no question but the Queene must for many reasons come by Worcester [both to avoide Essex and those forces at Coventree, Northampton, and Warwick as alsoe that she may finde a reasonable force there and a good resting place] and if we doe lye at Bister or thereabouts they cannot march to Worcester but you may be before them I shall enlarge there reasons when I have the honor to waite uppon you which I intend shall be tomorrowe if you come not to us, the same reason keepes the King from writing makes my letter much shorter that is my dispatch to the Queene. the King sent me this note just now : I have obeyed you in all things but money, and the reason of my disobedience in that is because it is not in my power and other cause then that I will never have for not obeying you being resolved eternally to be

        Your High^s

29th 4 of   Most humble and faithfull Servant
  the clocke   H. PERCY.

[No. 40.]

Sir

    There is another expresse come from the Queene this day by whom we are assured she will begin her journey this day or tomorrowe she comes certainely to Ashby but from thence we know not as yet which way she will take but some designe they have by the way the lesse the better, 3000 foote and 30 troopes of horse and dragons are all she marches with except such force as she may gett by the way, this I thought fitt to let you know and for want of this I shall suply it with making repetions to you how much satisfaction I have in telling you there is no creature in the world more yours than

    Your Hig^{nes} most humble
       and faithfull Servant
           H. PERCY

Oxford the 30 [April 1643]
  6 of the clocke

I hope we shall not have reason to complaine of our quarters.

[No. 41.]

S^r

  I could not possible put our traine in such a readinesse as to be able to march before 12 of the clocke and then the King receaved a letter from my Ld Generall by which he desired the Cannon should not march if they were not advanced already which hath staied me for the present so that now I doe attend what other orders I shall have, that being the cause I doe not waite uppon you as my inclinations doe invite me to having noe greater satisfaction then the giving you proofes that I am

    Your Hig^{nes} most humble Servant
          HEN PERCY

Oxford 8 June [1643]

The King will be extreamely glad to heere what you intend & as soone as I knowe the Cannon is not likely to marche I will presently waite uppon you

[No. 42.]

[c 3 July 1643

S^r

We have receaved news just now by a letter that comes from the North that Bradford is taken with all the men, armes and ammunition that were in it only Fairefax and his sonne escaped by night to Leeds, but this does not come so certainely as to be built uppon—Waller and your Brother with both armyes are mett, we have newes from them but it is soe uncertaine of both sides as I know not what to beleeve until wee heere of something more perfect : Your letter is come now to the King the messenger will be dispatched againe this night. I have not spoken with the King therefore I cannott say any thing to you of it, but I shall never be weary of saying to you that I will eternally be

   Your High^{ns} most humble humble Servant

        H. PERCY

I doe humbly begg of you that you will beleeve there is a necessity for my being heere, other wise I could not endure this.

[No. 43.]

SIR

The last night I did fully resolve to have waited uppon you this day having as much impatience to performe that duty as is possible for any creature to have.—But I am diverted from this by a commaund the King hath given me this day of being ready to march with all his traine of Artillery upon a short warning which is not to be done without my being present heere and the supplye of moneyes which I am promised every howre but cannott gett. I hope S^r this excuse being soe just in itself and soe displeasing to me I hope you will not only free me from all kind of condemnation but have some little pitty for what I suffer in being from you. I hope you are satisfied with those things I sent you. Since I was conjured by you to silence I could not say one word to 175 of △ designe therefore I doe not know what motions it hath or whether it doe continuw or noe. I think it is excellently laid and I hope will have a happy successe, if 237 doe send a regiment and 1000 foote ☐ 27, 32, 26, 38, 52, 39, 23, 50, either send 163 or one that may be as fitt to do you service to 244 let me know by your next whether 163 may say anything to 175 of it because there may be somethings that may concerne this buisnesse may require the motions and assistance of a servant, for you know very well when he doth things alone they are commonly crooked or untoward therefore let me know your sence in this for without it I shall not doe anything. My Ld Willmotts' regiment went to towne according to the K^s instruction but found noe body there, for those troopes that we thought to have found there were gone away at three of the clocke in the afternoon soe they returned without doing anything Mr. Harding is come out of the West and Co^l Kirke can tell you what newes he brought with him My Lieut^{nt} Coro^n-ll is in greate haste to be gone and for feare that resoultion may change I will only adde to this that I am Your High^{nes}

     Most humble humble Servant
          H. PERCY.

Oxford 6 July [1643]

[No. 44.]

SIR

  I receaved both your letters but am resolved to thank you for neither chusing rather to acknowlege them to be above anything that I can say then to make a triall and say too little. Your sending for a Cyfer is a just reproach to my providence, for I should have thought of it my selfe, but I conceave it a sufficient punishment for this fault that for want of it I have mist the contentment I should have had of knowing your thoughts these 2 dayes past, which I valew more then any thing can be given me; and I only begg of you that I may receave them constantly until I change that opinion. I never sawe anything of writing more sutable to you then then the 2 lines where you say you doubt not of ruining Essex his army, if noe greate misfortune happen [which I know you too well to feare]. It is very apparent that honor and a court agrees very well together for there was never any body made [from being the least courtier] soe greate a one as 214 by being a Lord, I hop eit will have influence soe farre as to make him pay that to you which he hath not exceeded in that is his obedyence Conwallis went away to the Queene the King did not write by him [I did] which was a little recommendation of his owne person which you know I am well acquainted withall— We have heard noething since I writt last of the Queene, from the West, now the horse that were sent for from Exeter are come they doe intend to march towards Waller. Rather than goe to Church yesterday in the afternoone I chose to goe to see the Cap. whoe I found very solitary in his little house. I stayed there till 6 of the clocke and going away I receaved this injunction from him to tell you that he is very much your servant and extreamely desires to have the honor to see you without which he will never goe away, and this I did promise to say in my first letter. I am very glad to heere you begin to be reconciled to Sunday but I desire you never to be to the day of the Lord. For my Lieut^t

Cor¹ I shall shewe myselfe very charitable to him with your assistance, not having strong dispositions to goodnesse myselfe but with some helpe you shall see for this matter I shall behave myselfe well, but I will ask none of any creature to give you all the proofes in the world that I am pleased with noe thing more then the beeing and telling your Hignesse I am

     Your most humble Servant

        H. PERCY.

Oxford

 I hope you will lett me have a quarter for I intend to waite uppon you within a day or 2 but let not that keepe you from writing if you have anything to commaund me.

[No. 45.]

Sʳ

 My Lᵈ of Richmond did acquaint me with the letter you writt to him last in which I finde the cheefe businesse was want of money, I did not only apply myselfe to make the Kinge forward in this supply, but to advance it I lent Ashburnham £300 to make up that proportion you desired. I hope there is noe danger you will belive this a Courtship to him but an extreame desire in me you should want noething that I may help you unto You know how greate want we have of Powder and what mischeefe that may bring uppon us if not timely prevented, the which I see few either goes about or can find out, the Parliament have there greatest works of Guilford there mills, are 2 miles from thence not guarded at all, or soe slenderly as they may be easily surprised for which purpose I doe goe with my owne regiment and 150 Dragoons if this succeed it will be a very good service to his Ma^ty and consequently acceptable to you, there is noe force neerer that place then London. We expect daily to heere you are in Bristowe—Waller is gone as fast as he can to London to complaine of my L^d of Essex for betraying of him which he will have soe much reason for as the Houses certainly will resent it highly this will cause much distraction in there affaires and I hope we shall take the advantage of it, and you returne to this place as soone as you can I have noe thing more to say to you but that I am and ever will be

Your High^ns most humble Servant

H. PERCY.

22nd Oxford
    [July 1643]

[No. 46.]

S^r

I am now going away yet heering that there is one going to you I cannott let him passe without saying some wot. The Queene's health doth begin to mend which is a greate blessing to us all, the King hath desired her to imploy herselfe to make you Wilmott and Culpeper frends and the like to all the rest of us, she thinks it fitt to be done for the present as the K^s affaires stand and soe do I to; what you think I hope I shall know when I waite uppon you and then I shall entertaine your Highnesse at large of this matter and adde only this now that I am satisfied extreamely with what the Queene doth in my perticuler and no lesse in saying to you I am infinitely your High^es

Most humble humble Servant

H. PERCY.

I beseech you let noe
body see my letters

23 July [1643]

[No. 47.]

S^r

Though you seemed not to be pleased that I should hope for the taking of Bristowe before it was soe, which fault I confesse I doe not understande, Yet I hope you will give me leave to congratu with you now amongst the rest of those that wish you all kind of happinesse the taking of that place. My L^d of Dunsmore will informe you perticulerly of all the passages heere concerning the disputes that are amongst you where you are. I arrived heere but yesterday and since that have not bin negligent in pressing those things I did beleeve you desired, and your old good frends have bin as dilligent pournous faire des riches the perticulers I shall tell you heere after. Your best frends doe wish that when the power is put absolutely into your hands you will comply soe farre with the Kings affaires as to doe that which may content many, and displease fewest; your successe in armes I hope will not make you forgett your civility to Ladyes this I say to you from a discourse the Queene made to me this night wherein she told me she had not receaved one letter from you since you went though you had writt many which is a fault you must repaire. I shall stay heere now therefore commaund me as you use to doe which will be a grate satisfaction to me that am

Your Highⁿ most humble Servant

H. PERCY

Let me know if you write to the Queene and receave instructions what to say

Oxford the 29th
[July 1643]

[No. 48.]

Oxford 30 [July 1643]

S^r

I writt to you yesterday I can say little more of your affaires then what I did because we doe expect both my Lo^d of Harford's comming to this place and my Ld Dunsmores returne before we shall either discourse or act anything that you know not already, for that I writt of the Queene I hope you will give her noe more the advantage to lay that fault to your charge; my cheefe buisnesse to you now is to obey the K'^s commaunds whoe spoke to me to desire you to send me an exact account of cannon and all sort of armes and ammunition that is there that accordingly the provisions necessary for his Ma^{ty} service may be made. S^r the carts and horses I sent from hence are very much wanted heere there being none almost left for the bringing in those dayly provisions that are necessary for the supplying of this place, and you were pleased to promise they should be returned in tow dayes; I have noe thing more to say to you but that I am and will ever be

Your Hig^s most humble Servant

H. PERCY

You will guesse at the reason of this bearers comming let me know what you desire your Servant to doe.

I had an expresse commaund to present the Duchesse of Richmonds service to you

The King is likely to come to you shortly It is said heere you are not carefull of your foote but have lost many since the taking of the towne.

[No. 49.]

May it please your Ma^{ty}

My Ld Generall did speake this morning with one of the Ingeneers whoe told him what I writt to yr Ma^{ty} I was not there at the same time myselfe but he desired me to acquaint your Ma^{ty} with those perticulers that soe you might have a good measure of the condition of your affaires heere, yet uppon a further enquiry, I find the Ingineere deceaved himselfe and caused that of my Lo^d Generalls, but if there be any mistake in this now they are all to be blamed having concurred in what I shall say to you M^{ty}

They find the moate to be 12 foote deepe and neere 30 broade, and if they goe on this way of casting earth before them it will be a weeke before they passe their gallery, but if they take away there blinds and bring men to cast fagotts only under the favor of our Musqueteers that must play uppon them continually whilst we are working it will be passed in 2 nights with the losse of men and the expense of much powder, they are resolved to continue the first way for this night and cast as many fagotts as they can my Lo^d Generall expecting to receave further order from Y^r Ma^{ty} when he shall waite

I

uppon you. S^r for what concerns me it will be very fitt that I give you a timely account [seeing this buisnesse hath and may drawe into a greater length than was imagined] of the proportione of powder that hath bin spent and what is remaining, that soe your Ma^{ty} may not be surprised with our want of ammunition but that there may be order taken for supplies for every day this expense is likely to increase as we approach neerer, there hath bin spent as I shall be able to make appeere in perticulers 120 barrells at least and there are remaining 70 the uncertainety of what I heard of your comming made me venter to send away this bearer, the other Ingeneere was not very willing to come and I doe beleive this the fitter for your service I have noe thing to adde to this but that I am

          Your Ma^{tys}
      Most obedient subject and Servant
                        H. PERCY

Camp
   17th Aug^t [1643]

[No. 50.]

S^r

    There is already arrived at Bristow 100 barrells of Powder and 200 musketts which I beleeve will be fitt to be sent away when your regiment marches, the rest shall come directly to Oxford the neerest way and from thence I will send them presently to Worcester and from thence to your Hig^{nes} If there be anything else heere or within my commaund you desire I shall most willingly obey your commaunds as soone as I receave them In the meane time I will only trouble your Hig^nes with the assurance that I am

>Your most humble Servant
>
>>PERCY

Oxford the 17th

Sir

I beseech you that it will please you to returne those carts and horses I sent uppon your commaund.

[No. 51.]

S^r

I receaved your letter and in obedience to your commaunds I have sent away those things your Hignesse agreed on with me such only excepted as are not in our Stores or in the hands of the Comissioners whose will we must waite uppon for the Match Our Pioneers are very few and we have sent away soe many gunners and mattrosses to Redding your Hignesse and my Ld Hopton as we have not men sufficient to employ for the ordinary dutyes of the magazine, and materialls we have not one. My Ld Hopton and Sr J. Ashley are to joyne this day at Kingscleere and will give on uppon the enemy this day or to-morrow morning they will be joyned 3000 foote and as many horse. If there be anything else I can serve your Hignesse in I shall doe it as

>Your Hig^se most humble servant
>
>>PERCY

Oxford the 15^t
Novem^r (1643)

This letter come to my hands being sent by my Ld Salton whoe was taken at Newbery

[No. 52.]

S[r]

I have receaved yours of the 21st of Feb[r] by which I doe perceave your Hignesse is displeased with a warrant sent from the King to his store keeper at Bristowe beleeving it was procured by me in prejudice of the comaund of your Hignesse, I doe protest to you there is noe such matter neither did I beleeve S[r] that I had lost soe much of your favor as that any body could make you have a suspition of me for that, when your Hignesse hath seene me uppon severall occasions give you all demonstrations that might make you be confident noe creature wished your commaunds more entire and absolute than I. S[r] I did desire the King uppon the writing of your letter before my L[d] Germoin that he would referre the consideration of this to his privy councell. I not desiring to meddle at all with it and soe I left it. S[r] For your amunition and armes I was to send your Hignesse I hope I shall give you such an account as you will cleerley see there was noe neglect in me neither can I yet see where the imstake was or by whom, for Mr. Russell can tell your Hignesse how I called uppon him before Ar Trevor for settling that soe as it might goe along with him and sent my warrants away for that intent for 100 barrells of Powder and all the musquetts were then there which were 400 and since another warrant for 100 more of our new ones which I beleeve much fitter than the others the first parcel I did beleeve had bin with your Hignesse till I heard the contrary lately and uppon my faith cannot accuse myselfe of any omission therein. If I did I would ingeniously confess it to your Hignesse and desire both your pardon and his Ma[tys] for one cannot offended in this without the other. For the residue of that proportion the King promist you there will be some tyme required for the performance for there are Comissions for presses gone out to the Sheriffs for 6000 men and I doe assure you S^r we have not as yet above 1000 armes for this, and I have an express comaund not to issue out armes till most of these recreuts are provided. Therefore you may S^r by this see what a condition the Kings necessityes put mee into that I must of necessity disobey heere or else incurre your displeasure which I will avoide with as much care as any servant you have, what soe ever my Ld Hopton desires he must have en despit de moy. S^r for the pouder was sent to Dudley Castle it was sent without bullett the Comissioners making answer there was none, my Ld Germin knowes this was the truth and noe kind of fault in me S^r as I have taken the liberty now to justify myselfe not to have bin guilty of any neglect to you or your service soe I beseech you to give me leave alsoe to tell you S^r I cannot beleeve them your reall servants that doe give you jealousies of those that doe not deserve them therefore S^r with all the confidence that an honest man can have I doe desire you will be pleased to think me entire in this justification and ready likewise in all things you will comaund me to shew your Hig^{nes} that I am extreamely

   Your Hig^{ness}
     Most humble Servant
        PERCY

Oxford the 21 March [1643-4]

I beseech you S^r doe me the favour to let me heere from you if there remaine any kind of insatisfaction towards me.

[No. 53.]

S^r

I hope your Highnesse hath receaved one of mine before this time where I have represented to you cleerlely that there hath bin noe fault in my orders towards your service. I sent 20 barrells of Pouder to Dudley Castle with match but noe bullets for there was none, and I heere the amunition and armes from Bristowe is safely arrived at Worcester and there is order taken heere to send one that may take care for the speedy advancing it toward to Shresbury. This is what I can say for the present and for the future what soe ever commaunds you lay uppon me I am confident I shall give a most perfect account of my obedience to them. I cannot close up this letter without telling your Hignesse I am one of those that doe congratulate with you your most happy victory both as it increaseth your owne glory and as it hath raised his Maj^{ties} affaires to a greater height of prosperity than any body could have imagined at this time this is a subject would give me a greate latitude to write off but my Lo^d Jermin will not therefore I conclude with this request that you will be pleased to thinke me as I have often professed to be

Your Hig^{nes} most humble Servant,

PERCY.

Oxford the 28th [March 1644]

[No. 54.]

S^r

I have read your lettter and that of Sr Lewis Dives I hope the vexation that you have had will shew his Mat^y so perfectly the mischiefes that are likely to fall out uppon such orders as caused this that the like may be avoided for the time to come and your Hig^nes never put to this againe, we are to meete this afternoone and soe we shall doe every day to consider of all things that may be for your honor and his Mat^tys service in which you shall never finde any creature more neerely concerned then

    S^r

   Your most humhle Servant

       PERCY.

Oxford 28 [Mar : 1644]

[No. 55.]

Fragment of a letter from Lord Percy.

175 hath receaved a letter from 244 that he lies at Cosill this night but does not say expressly what way he will take but leaves it to conjecture, which is an omission, you will heere the relation of it from 175. 163 hath asked leave of 175 to come to 237, but he did absolutily refuse it upon this ground that if he should have occasion to march the Artillery would be in greate disorder. 132 intended to have come along with me but he is prevented. 163 did moove 175 that he would commaund 214 expressly to come away for I knew very well by some heere the contrary was intended by him, and I doe quarrell with you for not writing anything of it to me; That 224 hath sent for Newport by whome they doe beleeve to kindle a new that mutinous fire which was a dying but I doe beleeve it will not be to much purpose yet you may make use of it if you please; Wee have no certaine newes from the West which is a most strange thing; My Lo^d of Essex wee heere is marching backe towards Alsbury which I think

the neerest way to his destruction: all the newes out of North is confirmed and Leedes taken soe that we conceave all the North absolutely ours. I doe humbly desire you that you will commaund your Secretary to give those officers of mine Commissions that have none that soe they may not be taken out of my regiment nor your Brigade by others that perhaps may pretend to them by guift from my Ld Newcastle; for myself let me never have other then that which you give me to intitle me to be ever

        Your Hig^{nes}
          Most humble humble Servant
                  H. PERCY

Oxford 8th July
  [1643]

ANALYSIS OF LETTERS & DOCUMENTS
(apparently prepared by Col. Benett.)

[No. 56.]

The Breviates of the Princes letters

Towcester	Sr A. Aston saw the workes on the hill begun
Novemb 22, 1643	Denbigh goes thorow Northampton; Essex sends men in to Ailesbury & Northampton desires ayd ag^t him; for fear of Towcester but some of P. R. troopes sent away ere now & Aston expects to be called out Sr John Byron's horse were quartered at Brackley & Willmott who went sick to Oxford Novemb 8 1643
Octob 30	About October 30 Thelwell comes from Reding towards Towcester wth 600 ffoote, 900 more being sent back. Willmot lay then at Buckingham. More forces sent into Ailesbury about mid November wch on Saturday 18 mustered 1400 by poll: & Essex marcht that waye.
Worcester Estate in April 1643	Worcestershire Commissioners doe little for King pretending to be hindered by Sr W. Russell's differences. Gilb Gerard Governor there. The Countryes contribution, 3000l a month, Jan. 22, 1643
Tillier & Broughton 11 February 1643	landed with 1800 ffoote & Sr W. Vaugham wth 300 horse: whome L Byron sent to Shrewsbury They are at Ruthen Febr 21

Towcester Nov. 7 1643	Ld Biron from Brackley sends in Showells Spades &c
Ld Biron intended to be made Generall of Lancashire: desires first to be made Pr Charles Governor.
March 14 1642 Pyms letter	P. R having gone to Bristoll, Essex sends forces to Tame: but recalls them upon the Princes returne: They consulted at Westminster about a cessation: but agreed not, Shortly came the Treaters to Oxford
1643 Jan. 14	Sr Nicholas Byron & Sr R. Willis taken.
Ailesbury	Some messages betwixt the Governor & Lord Biron then at Brackly November 9, 1643 but upon the fayling of Newport Pannell he sends Biron's woman messenger to Essex then at St Albans
Newark 1644	Upon the taking of this. Bellassys from Yorke sending into the Ile of Axholme, the Rebells quitt it in Maye 1644
Ailesbury March 19, 1642	Sr John Culpeper's letter was ag^t correspondence with towne and ag^t the hopes: but Prince being marcht, the designe was knowne at Oxford
Camp removed	Forth writes to the King that Essex meanes to quarter in Buckinghamshire & advises to rayse Abingdon leaguer & quarter the soldiers betwixt Whately & Oxford in Barnes & villages.
Shropshire Estate	Lord Capell complaynes that by drawing away the P of Wales regiment from him his

condition was so weakened that the Rebells planted at Draiton : professes that w^h 2000 ffoote more to take Warwick and Stafford : Invites P. R to looke that waye, being confident that there was no part of the Kingdome where in so short a time so much advantage may be made, & 6000 horse & ffoote raysed to marche any whither, nor a greater oportunity to add another Trophy to his Highnesse glorious atchievements Writes to invite the Prince again Aprile 14.

Latham
March 7, 1643

E of Derby invites the Prince to take Liverpoole & releeve Latham : assuring his presence would strike terror into the Rebells & new life in the good subjects. Tells him in a former letter upon P. R his coming to Shrewsbury. That his fame getts credit to his Servants.

Lincoln
April 11, 1644

The state of Licolne after Newark taken : expressed by 11 Commissioners letter.

Yorkshire
March 29, 1644

Theyre Commissioners desire the Princes help : in 2 letters March 29, April 1.

Denbighshire
1644.

After the Prince was gone to Shrewsburye to settle the County, quarters & contributions : See how backward the Commissioners of Arraye are for the mayntenance of one onely regiment of R. Ellices.

Newark
1643, Jan 31

The Commissioners of Lincolne & Nottinghamshire expresse their charges, feares of seige, the Scots invasions Newcastle's fortifying Doncaster, & drawing away of Sr C. Lucas & other forces to resist them.

Bellassys allso complaynes he is calling out of York by Newcastle.

<small>Newark Aprile 26, 1644</small>

E. of Newcastle in streights. The Newark Commissioners invite the Prince to releive him.

<small>1643 October 2</small>

Glamorgan thanks the Prince for diswading him to marche into Cheshire: & gives him reasons why he since came to Tewksbuyre.

<small>Bristoll Maye 27 1643</small>

Essex writes to Fiennes—I hope ere this you have made some examples of the Bristoll Traytors; & put others to a fine & ransome.

<small>Armes to Bristoll</small>

The Queen sends a Dunkirk frigate wth Armes pistolls Shott Granadoes etc to Bristoll Aug 15, 1643.

<small>Bristoll fort</small>

Greate fort at Bristoll begun. Hopton desires the Princes order in it Sept 1, 1643 Hopton desires the Prince Hawly may be his Leiftenant Governor

<small>1643 Feb 12 Ld Digby's compliments.</small>

Ld Digby professes all faythfullnesse to the Princes service: beseeching him to be confident that no man living should bring more industrye or more affection to the execution of all his commands then he should, when the Prince should honor him wth them.

<small>April 6 1644</small>

And Whereas it seems by other of Digby's letters, there was a purpose at Oxford to recall the Prince thither from Shrewsburye,

P. R. by Kgs orders continued at Shrewsburye

presently after his Newark victorye: and one order had been sent from the King by Digby; And Whereas the Prince was desirous to continue in Shropshire till he could gett up an Armye, the King sends other orders by Digbye, Dated April 6, 1644, upon that Digby thus complements. That the prince should stay there to rayse such an armye, as wee shall not neede committ that wch you esteeme a fault any more, of relying upon your reputation, which though it be not a foundation for councells, & resolutions; yet you must be pleased to allowe it to be of excellent heartning to all those who have so high an opinion of your virtue and braverye, as possesses the heart of y^r Highnesse most affectionate Servant

GEORGE DIGBY

Oxford April 6, 1644

1642 March 31 Essex agst peace

It seemes presently after Edgehill, there was some private designe to have Warwick Castle delivered: wherefore Essex would not lett Col Vavasor be sent Prisoner thither. Essex extreme obstinate agaynst peace, as out of hope of pardon (says Lady Aubigny)

1643 Apr. 18

Goring testifyes, the Queene understoode & esteemed P. R beyond his expressions

The North Aprile 22 1643

Goring writes Newcastle was 16000 strong well armed: whereof neere 3000 horse besides dragooners: & 2000 more new levyed ffoote, yet unarmed.

1643 Sept 17	The King by Digby to the Prince : pursuing Essex from Glocester : & Rupert having overtaking Essex : the King desires to know where to bring up the ffoote to him
Shropshire Nov 7 Decr 12 1643	Byron to be sent to Lancashire. It seems Ormond had sent some into Cheshire, wch he called his Armye Cheshire could march 4000 ffoote & neere 1000 horse besydes Capels in Shropshire sayes Ld Byron : Harding Castle taken by them upon composition.
Jan. 14 Byron : Nantwich	Byrons designe on Nantwich retarded by Fairfaxes, coming to releeve it took some of Fairfaxes Sr N. Byron & Willys taken wth 8 Cornells—Ernely commes hopes to take Nantwich
Feb 21	Broughton Tillier & Vaughan landed & sent towards Shrewsburye
Feb 24	Fairfaxes accompt of Cheshire
Aprile 4, 1643	Estate of Cheshire & Shropshire at Ld Capell's coming
14	He invites the Prince thither ; he invites the Prince again
Shropshire	Lancashire & Cheshire in Capells April 4 1643. Brereton Sir W. Fairfaxes accompt. Brereton besieged in his howse : able to hold out for 6 or 7 dayes Feb 20 1643, 1642 Broughton & Tillier w^c 1800 by list & Sr W. Vaughan wth 300 horse landed about time, of princes setting out of Oxford. These sent to Shrewsburye

March 2 1643 March 23 Newark.	Latham besiged : see Byron's letter. The Prince going to Newark left Byron at Chester, & ordered a partye of horse to go releive Latham, sayes Derby's letter but by March 23 they were too close about the house.
March 7	See Derbye's letter
Newark Sollicites forayd Jany 31 State of it and Lincolnshire	Axholme quitt, whence Meldrum forced Sr John Magney & his horse about Jan : 24, 1643—a little before this gatt they Gainsborow. Sr Charles Lucas sent to the North (after Towcester) called to Doncaster. Lincoln when taken.
April 1 1644	See Commissioners letters Jan 31 Lincoln & Gainsborow quitt. Porter called away by Newcastle—Commissioners of Lincolne
April 9	Lincoln Estate Crowland beseiged.
April 26	State of the North. Implore Princes ayd April 1 & March 29 then Newcastle offers prince the command.

LETTERS FROM WILLIAM BENETT TO HIS MOTHER, MRS. BENETT, NORTON BAVENT.

[No. 57.]

Hon^d Mother

I had writt to you as soone as I came to Towne but y^t I thought you would have y^e newes of y^e progation of ye Parliam^t before my letters could come to y^r hands; but now there is some latter newes wch praps you have not heard, & y^t is a second pte to ye olde tune of Shameing ye Plott; by suborneing of Wittnesses to sweare severall things whereby to asperce & cast an odium on ye Duke of Monmouth & severall other Peeres, thereby to lighten ye burthen of ye Papist Lords, ye pticulers of ye story I cannot give you, but this is certaine y^t Mr Christian one y^t belongs to ye Earl of Danby is taken into custody, & it is s^d y^t Blood is likwise apprehended, for ye same fact wth three or fowre more, this is all at psent, with my humble duty to yor self & due respects to all my relations, wisheing all happinesse to attend you, I take my leave & remain

Your most dutifull Sonn

WM. BENETT

Jan 31st
  1679

[No. 58.]

Hon^d Mother

This last weeke I writ to you to desire a returne

for some money, but now you need not send any bill, for Mr Cray is in towne & I shall be supplyed by him. I doe thinke to begin my journey towards you on Thursday ye 16th instant, (if I can make ready y^r businesse by y^t tyme) therefore I would have my horse to meet me at Basingstoake on y^t day, if you doe not heare from me to ye contrary, by ye next post. This day ye King in Councell declared ye Parliam^t to be desolved, & y^t a new one shall meet ye seventh of October. Heare have ben a report y^t there was an attempt made upon ye King's pson to kill him, at Windsor, but I thinke there is little truth in it: if you heare of a small Prophett y^t is lately come to towne, about 3 years old, & three foot high, y^t can speake all languages as you may take my word for it, y^t it is a lye, for, there is noe more in it but this, ye father or some other pson soe soone as ye childe could speake hath taught it some few words of Latine & Greeke. Thus wth my duty to yor self and kinde respects to all my relations, I take leave & remaine

    Yo^r most dutifull Sonn

       WM. BENETT

July ye 10th,
 1679
These
  ffor his honor^d mother
  Mrs. Elizabeth Benett at
  Norton Bavent nere
  Warminster Wilts.

[No. 59.]

Hon^d Mother

  Yesterday in ye afternoone I came to London,

my journey was something stormey untill I came to Gosper nere Portsmouth, wch is a place lately fortified both ags^t ye land & sea. Y^e sea forts lyes conveniently to impede ye passage of ships y^t shall come into ye harbor beyond Portsmouth & ye land works may serve to secure those forts if any enemy should land at ye back of them. Portsmouth itselfe is very strong and they are hard at work to make it stronger. I suppose you have heard of ye Parliamts being prorogued untill ye 26th of January. The People talks very loude of these often putting off of Parliamts & seeme to be much discontented. It is said y^t the Duke of York is to goe for Scotland next Twesday, this day he went into ye Citty to dyne there, wth the Artillery men at there accustomed feast, & hereby he may easily pceave ye affections of ye People towards him, for as he passed through Cheapeside ye multitude gazed at him, but did not soe much as shew him ye respect of putting off their hats, this the newest newes of ye towne y^t I can entertaine you wth at p^{r}sent, therefore shall take my leave & wth my humble duty to yor self and kinde respects to all my relations. Wisheing you health & happinesse I remain

    Yo^r most dutifull Sonn

      WM. BENETT

October ye 20th [or 27th]
 1679

[No. 60.]

London No^{ber} y 6th 1679

Hon^d Mother

 There have been lately a greate discovery made

of y ͤ fained Presbiterian plott y ᵗ was soe much buss'd about in ye Country; ye noise whereof, I beleeve is sufficiently spread into all pts of y ͤ nation; the Papists intending thereby to through off ye odium of theire plott from themselfs, thought to cast it upon y ͤ Presbiterians; for w ᶜʰ purpose they used these artifisses; first to seduce y ͤ Kings evidence, viz. Mr Dugdall,* a man of y ͤ most unblemished reputation of all y ͤ discoverers, & sollicited him w ᵗʰ y ͤ promise of greate rewards, to recant all y ᵗ he had given in evidence ag ᵗ y ͤ preists & Jesuits he resolveing to finde out y ͤ depth of there designe lead them on with hopes; but w ᵗʰ all imparted the affaire to severall psons of quality who at y ͤ meeteings of Dudgall and Pasborough (whoe was ye man y ᵗ sollicited him) were placed, soe in private corners, y ᵗ they might heare ye discourse, but meeteing w ᵗʰ severall delayes Pasborough did begin to be jealous of Dugdall; whereupon, he found out some means to acquainte y ͤ King & Councill, y ᵗ Dugdall offered to recant, for a sume of money; thereby, thinkeing to disparage his evidence: but upon examination Dugdall was cleared in his reputation; and Pasborough comitted to Newate & to back this stratagem there was another devise, & as it was to be acted after y ͤ other had taken effect, soe it happened to be discovered miraculously in y ͤ like order, they haveing poynted out severall psons for destruction whom they thought was ag ᵗ there interest, both of ye nobility and gentry, in

---

* Burnet says of Dugdale * * * "This" (the behaviour of the condemned Papists on the scaffold) "began to shake the credit of the evidence, when a more composed and credible person came in to support it. One Dugdale, that had been Lord Aston's bailiff, and lived in a fair reputation in the country, was put in prison for refusing the oaths of allegiance and supremacy."—Burnet's 'Own Times,' vol. i. p. 444, edit. 1724.

order hereunto, there was one Dangerfeild* alias Willoby, y^t came to a house where one Collonell Mansell lodged, & took up lodgeings for himselfe, & haveing in a short tyme an opptunity to goe into ye Collonells chamber, when he was out of ye way, under ptence of seeing it; placed some letters of treasonable matters behinde his bed; and then goes to ye costome house & informes ye officers, y^t there was in this Mansells chamber phibited goods to ye value of 2000l. & bring them to search, but they not findeing any such goods, this informer, wished them to looke behinde ye bed, where immediately they found ye fores^d papers wch being carried to ye Councell Mansell was sent for & upon examination of ye matter ye cheat was discovered & the informer sent to prison * * * * * it is s^d have discovered ye whole affaire now in the middest of these * * * * * * * * * happened that Sr William Waller had some item or suspition that there might be something of moment in one Mrs. Selliers house where the St Omers witnesses lodged & in searcheing found in the bottom of a meale tub a booke wch is a compendium of the whole designe & about 2 dayes since he found out more of Harcortes papers with a legier booke, y^t confirmeth ye truth of ye first plott. In this last villanous contrivance it is s^d that Sir Robert Paten whoe is elected K^t of Parliam^t for Midd is deeply concerned & it was farther designed y^t Blood whoe stole ye Crown, should be first seised & accused for designeing to kill ye King, whoe for ye sake of his pardon should impeach all those y^t they had designed for destruction, & when this was don ye King should be

* "Dangerfield, a subtle and dexterous man, who had gone through all the shapes and practices of roguery, and in particular was a false coiner, undertook now to coin a plot for the ends of the Papists."— Burnet's 'Own Times,' vol. i. p 475.

on a sudden made away; I doe not heare y^t there is any evidence ag^t. Blood or y^t he is secured. Ye Lady Powis is comitted for being an abettor in this plott, & soe is ye Ld Castlemaine. Haveing noe more at psent I shall take my leave wth my humble duty to yor self & kind respects to all my relations & remaine

    Yo^r most dutifull Sonn
        WM. BENETT

LETTERS FROM

WILLIAM BENNETT

TO

COLONEL BENETT.

[No. 61.]

LETTERS FROM WILLIAM BENNETT TO COLONEL BENETT.

From Sturmister Mill.
Oct° ye 1, 77

Dear Cosin

Tho ffarr hath now brought the good newes that Oberton writeinges are found; he will give you a ffarther account of that. Cosin a peice of land that I very well know, is now to be sold, all good pasture ground & noe doubt in the title I always tooke it to be under set at least 10l. per ann : it lyes in Marnhull parish, yet but a mile from Margrett Marsh, I suppose nothinge can be bought that wil be more certaine of a good tenant, to take any time what soever, & noe danger of payment of ye rent, it is one Mr. Joanes land of Lime a very rich man, & right honest worthy gentleman, he did not set it to sale, but I desired Mr Burbidge his brother in Law to aske him whether he would part with it, he have sent me a price, & I shall speake with him myselfe next weeke about it, the value of ye land as now set is a hundred & five pounds per ann. S^r yf you have noe desire to purchese, I doe by noe meanes endeavor to pswade you unto it; yet pray give mee a line by ye very next post, in answere unto this, yf it be noe kindnesse unto you a freind of mine I very well know will gladly accept it, you are to take notice y^t there is noe house on ye land, my most faithfull service p^{r}sented unto all my very good freinds, I meane those what went unto London with you.

for ever ye same whilst yor Unckell

WILL BENNETT

[No. 62.]

Shafton Octo ye 13. 77

Good Cosin

A wensday last I was at your ffarme at Codford, & the next morn: Jefery & I was there againe but to noe purpose at all; for Mr Ingrum & some others; have quite altered ye ffarmer last resolves for the errable that belongs to ye farme the Cow Lease & house was the only bargaine he now p^{r}ferred rent for, that I did not thinke fit to consent unto & soe we parted, he beinge willinge to speake with you about ye errable & Cow lease. Cosin I am told ye ffarmer Shephard of Litle Ambesbury, wants a ffarme at this instant of time for his Lanlord have sold that he now lives in, & ye purchaser comes to live in ye farme I have sent unto him about yor haveing some acquaintance with him myselfe the onely thinge I doubpt of yf it he comes to view your farme, is the very meanesse of your house & a stable not fit for any good cart horse to stand in, I thinke it wil be some what hard to gett a good sufficient tenant, to be pleased with ye house & much more dislike unto ye stable, I shall make it part of my buishnesse to set your ffarme against you come downe.

Sir

Your sistere Patience desires me to p^{e}sent her humble service to her freinds & shee likewise intreats my Bro. Matth: Bennett & your advice as in relation to Mr. Bishope & herselfe noe nuptiall vow is to be made, but with your good likeinge his estate I have seen about five hundred & fiftie pounds p an; engagements are not fit to be named on Letters, yf you please a line in answere is desired to her concerne. Jefery p^{e}sent his humble service, & desired me to satisfie my deare Cosen, & yo Lady with what she desired, sheepe bought at Shrowton 1080 at 10^s a peice more at Shrowton 40 at 7/6 a peice 10 shillinges giv^{en} back againe 100 sheepe from Stofton farme 11^s a peice 100 sheepe from ye farmer Turke 12^s a peice from John Imprum 80 sheepe 12^s a peice in the whole 500 sheepe 2 hundred sold from Codford at 14^s a peice the same

W. B.

[No. 63.]

East Orch, June ye 13, 78.

Dear Cosin,

I have yo^{rs} of ye 11 now before me, and Mr. Churchill or by his order shal be payd 100lb upon sight. Jeffrey Long is now with me, he canot returne you any mony, I have ordered him to bringe what mony he can make upp, unto Mr. Dibben and myself a Satterday next, wee will returne it unto you, (yf possible to be done) by Carryer, yf not otherwise.

Sir

I most heartily thank you, in relation unto your very kinde proferr, to doe my sone the honor as to be taken notice of, by soe very great psons (yf you please) pray doe not mention any thinge unto him, untill you here againe from me about it, yf it were possible to make him a prebend of Gloster, ye next turne y^t falls, noethinge soe good for him as I thinke.

I have spoken with Mr. Dibben alreadie about account, & will speake with him againe to morrow. I could wish Mr. Dibben was psnt when your account is stated, but he is very much imployed, & you best know whether Mr. White can well goe through with it.

S^r I sent you a lett: ye last weeke, I doe not finde by yo^{rs} that it came unto yo hand, it was to minde yo of 100*l*. I payd unto Mr. Dibben, which you pmised to pay, when I last saw you, & made my account with you, Tom ffarr being psent, and when I came to pay Mr. Dibben ye 100*l*. I was in your debpt, he told me he wanted y^r other 100*l*. also, & I payd that 100*l*. likewise, but without yo order & soe I borowed it. by reason Mr. Cheswell failed of payinge in mony to pay Mistris Pile, as you had ordered Mr. Dibben and myselfe to receive, I sent a lett about it 2 months since and mentioned ye same unto you, but rec^d no answere unto y^t pticular.

Mr. Bower have not payd his 100lb as yet by reason I had not ye mortgage I would not take it, I thinke he will pay in but 100*l*. of 200*l*. due, I have credit enough but forth of mony at present. My ffaithful service psented is all at psent from

    Your ever obliged Unckell,
      WILL BENNET.

. When the good Deane of Gloster comes unto London he wil be willing to doe any thinge in his power as to procure ye next grant for a prebend, but these are great favors, to hard I doubt for me to obtaine: my Bro. Matth once prmised to move the speaker in it.

[No. 64.]

    East Orch, Jann. ye 7, 78.

Deare Cosin,

 I rec^d yo^{rs} but this morn: Yo Mother hath taken Mr. Bury 300*l*. into her hands & taken it as her owne mony; but yf you write a line unto her, she will deliver ye 300*l.* unto Mr. Dibben & he will pay it as you shall give order. Coll. Butler mony is altogeather uncertaine when to be payd, yf you will be pleased to write unto him it is the better. Mr. Bower gave notice of paying in but 100^{li}.

S^r I did write unto you once before about a 100*l.* I payed unto Mr. Dibben for you, since we accounted… was 100*l.* of the 200*l.* I borrowed of Mr. Dibben to pay Mistris Pile the day when you went from Shafton, you & I accounted, Tom ffar being then p'sent, & there was 100*l.* then due unto you from me, which you ordered me to pay unto Mr. Dibben, & you then sayd you would take course to pay him ye other 100*l.* but when I came unto Mr. Dibben to pay my 100*l.* he told me that he had not rec^d ye 100*l.* of you, soe I payd him without yo order & borrowed ye 200*l.* likewise without yo order also, this I sett forth at length by reason you answered not a word unto that part of my lett: which was sent 3 weeks since yf you doe not remember it, I hope ye same account is to be found, I have it all upon my booke.

As to all other concerns in yo lett: I will most dilligently observe. Mr. Dibben is not at home but after I have rec^d yor next, a full account of what you have now written unto me about shall be given you, my ffaithfull service unto my good Cosin y^r Lady, for ever ye same whilst your Unckell.

WILL BENNETT.

Yf my good sister Matt^h
be with yo, pray p^{r}sent
my service unto her and
let know Capt. Blewcoate
is very well.

[No. 65.]

East Orch May y[e] 31 79

Deare Cosin,

In my last unto you I desired a kindnesse yf it lay in your way for my Unckell Mr John Snouk which is bearer hereof, he is a very honest man & I hope will pforme his duty well in any place he shall undertake, yf you can doe him any kindnesse, it wil be a very great favor unto him, & shall alwayes be acknoledged by

Yo[r] obliged Unckell &
Servuant
WILL BENNETT.

it is my L[d] Chancellor that have the gift of those pebends places at Gloster I onely minde it but doe not flatter myselfe that I have any hopes to p[e]vaile some of my Cosin D[s] freinds hath told me he will begin his shute againe, but I am told mony growes short with him. his wittnesses had mony before hand last time, yet his Bro. Roots his ffamily' is now kept most part by y[e] all parish Charitie & his other witnesse is sayd by all that knowes him that Lovell Winterburne nor any Weekes in Shafton can come neare him yf he be told his story right, he is your Bro. D[r] Baliffe at y[e] Devises & was sent by his master unto my house a purpose to know me & there was never a better Jury packed as Tom Beach that know them all sayes, & it cost him a great deale of mony, one of his Cabinett Consell hath told me all passages, & how Roots came to sweare I made y[e] pmise at Mr Davy house, where I never saw him; I think my Bro: was fully satisfied of Mr. Roots before those dayes & he was not likely to send me to treat with him. But as Mr. Eyers sayd he will sweare any thinge, yf he could but tell what will doe it, my service to yo Lady & my good Sister. W.B.

[No. 66.]

Shapton Ja y" 15 /80

Good Cosin

I rec^d noe answere unto my last letter pray be soe kind by ye next. I have now gotten a returne for yo 100*l*. and for a 100*l*. more for my Bro^r Matth Bennett use I have sent ye 200*l*. bill inclosed, pray send me Mr. Palmer receit for my 100*l*. rec^d for my Bro. Matth Bennett use, assone as he have rec^d ye mony. I am to mett your tenant at Salisbury Munday next, in order to ye settinge yo ffarme at Codford. 6 or 8 of yo very good freinds and myselfe am now drinkinge your good health in a glasse of good sacke. I want Mr. Palmer receit for ye fifteen pounds that yo. Bro. Burge rec^d of me. I mentioned ye same in my last, but want yo answere, Mr ffreke is now at home, I intend to wayte on him tomorrow my service unto all our freinds in hast from

Your obliged Unckell ye same

WILL BENNETT

[No. 67.]

Salisbury Ja ye 18/80

Deare Cosin

I was yeasterday with Col Butler (and I take him to be declininge apace as to his health) I modestly demaned yo 60*l*. due for interest for which he gave me a bond when he payd ye principall mony, he have pmised & failed me, from time to time this 12 months, & now he have named two dayes vizt Saterday come se night, 20*l*. and the rest at Lady day next I wish he may be well to pay both these payments himselfe, I will take what care in me lyeth about this concerne.

S^r I mett yo Codford tenant & Jeffery at Salisbury this day. Mr Tho Beach his wife beinge sicke could not come, after many words & longe winded discourses wee agreed. I have sett yo ffarme for three yeares for two hundred & sixtie pounds p ann. I have tyed ye ffarmer from shroudinge ye trees in ye home or less ffarme close, which ought to a been taken care of in his last lease, I have also made him release his psent right in ye shrowdes now growing on those trees, which are his owne by his lease I hope it wil be as well, as to keepe ye sheepe slight in hand, & now wee are not bound to keep a number of sheepe, at deere rates as formerly That was more than 10l. p ann. advance to the rent of ye ffarme you are to have securitie good enough for payment of rent.

I was Sunday last at Shrowton Mr. ffreke speakes very kindly, & affectionately of you he told me y^t you had spoken some what unto him about yo p^{r}sentation of Chesleborne parsonage yf you have a resolve to p^{r}sent him with it I wish would be soe kind as to send a letter directed unto him by Will Matth ye Caryer and ye p^{r}sentation also, that I may have ye favor to deliver it in yo name, it will come timely enough yf you send it to me by Matth. This returne you are to take notice by the bill I sent you now by Will Matth. Satterday next ye 200l. is to be called for

Yo Unckell ye same
WILL BENNETT.

[No. 68.]

Shafton, Ja ye 22/80

Deare Cosin

An answere unto yo^rs recd Thursday as I came from Salisbury (I sent you a lett from thence, my buishnesse there) I called at Shafton, and p^rsently my Bro^r Hurman & Mr. Mayor came and shewed me your Lett. they p^rsently went both of them downe to Mr. Wittaker, he answered as formerly, y^t yf ye towne thought fitt to chuse him, he was willinge to serve them, how farr y^t will p^rvaile I know not.

But wee thought it ye best way to send for 20 or 30 of our cheifest freindes & to make them acquainted with yo. intention to serve them againe yf they pleased; & I desired them to comuncate your intention to reste of all those y^t gave their voyces for you last time, this was our whole buishnesse Thursday afternoon, part of ye night, and Fryday & this morninge also; we finde them all, (save one) to stand very ffaithfully, & we have 10 or 12 voyces more than formerly.

This day I saw Sr Matth: Andrew's letter to Mr. Mayor, and he writes very kindly to his ffreindes, and intends to come and visitt them in pson. I am very confident noe one pson is able to stand in competion with you; but when Sr Matth And. comes and phapps treat high I am confident Mr. B. will court him to joyne with him; and this may putte us to trouble & charge and some hazard, pray consider you y^r part and weigh it very well.

S^r Wm. Murrell wayte on old Grove at fferne yeasterday, and they present their service unto you & nothinge shal be wantinge in them to doe you any service.

Wee have a speech about towne of Mr. ffownes to stand, but I give noe credit to that report as yet.

Mr. Graye recd a Lett. from my Ld of Shaftesbury* to this effect that, he thought Mr. Wittaker, and your selfe very fitt psons to serve ye Towne and Mr. Wittak

---

* At the period this letter was written Lord Shaftesbury was regarded as the leader of the Protestant party in the House of Lords. The Parliament had been dissolved on the 18th January, 1681 (1680, Old Style), and a new Parliament was summoned to be held at Oxford on the 21st March following. During the preceding session there had been stormy discussions upon questions of religion, the Popish Plot and the bill for excluding the Duke of York, on the ground of his religion, from his succession to the throne; and now Shaftesbury used every effort in his power for accomplishing the same objects. In Lord Shaftesbury's Life, by the late Mr. Christie, are to be found several traces both of Shaftesbury's action at this particular moment, and of his correspondence with Mr. Benett. On the former of these points it may be well to refer to some instructions which apparently were drawn up by him for the members of Parliament summoned at Oxford. They consisted of four heads :—" First, We all expect that you should, to the last, insist for a bill to exclude the Duke of York by name, and all other Popish successors, from coming to the Imperial Crown of this realm. Secondly, That you insist upon an adjustment to be made betwixt the King's prerogative of calling, proroguing, and dissolving Parliaments, and the rights of the people to have annual Parliaments to despatch and provide for those important affairs and business that can nowhere else be taken care of; for, without the certainty of Parliaments meeting in due distance of time from each other, and their sitting so long as shall be necessary for the despatch of the affairs of the nation, it is not possible but that our laws, liberties, lives, and estates should become in a short time at the will of the Prince. Thirdly, We expect you should restore us to that liberty we and our forefathers have enjoyed, until these last forty years, of being free from guards and mercenary soldiers; it being the inseparable right of a free nation that they themselves, and no separate number of paid or hired men, should have the guard of their own Prince, government, and laws. Lastly, Although we mention these three particulars as most necessary to us, yet there are several others of great importance which we leave to your wisdoms; assuring ourselves that, until you have fully provided for a complete security against Popery and arbitrary power, you will not give any of our money."

In January, 1678, Lord Shaftesbury wrote to his steward :—" You must remember to make up the account with Mr. Dibbons, and pay him

resolves as I understand not to spend any money; I am some what in doubt (altho he well deserves it) that will very hardly doe ye buishnesse effectually.

I hope you have rec^d my Salisbury Lett, and yf you intend to p^{r}sent our best freind with what I desired, pray let it be sent safe unto my hand, with you Lett. unto him I doe not feare his kindnesse in any pticular yf occasion require.

Vale
Yo Unckell ye same whilst
WILL BENNETT

I have just now seen
Sr Matth And: Letter
he doe not positively say
that he will come unto
Shafton

[No. 69.]

East Orchard, Ja ye 29. 80.

Deare Cosin,

Mr. Mayor and my Bro. Hurman was at Hargrove with me yeasterday; and wee had yo Munday letter before

the remainder of Mr. Bennett's interest money according to the note I gave you." And it will be seen, on reference to Letter No. 64, that Mr. Dibbon was in correspondence with William Bennett on monetary affairs. There is also, on the 28th August, 1675, a long letter from Lord Shaftesbury to Mr. Benett, giving an account of a quarrel which he had had with Lord Digby, arising out of the Shaftesbury election in that year. This letter will be found in the Appendix. It appears also that in a debate on the Exclusion Bill, Mr. Benett stated there "was no time to seek for means in the future: which must be understood and distant; and that it would be much surer and more advantageous if the King of England had already a son capable of succeeding him." This refers to Charles's natural son, the Duke of Monmouth, who, it was proposed by the extreme party, should be recognised as legitimate, and therefore as next heir to the throne. Mr. Benett spoke a second time in the debate—" If you will have the Duke of York come to the Crown, as other kings do, speak plain English. If you intend that, I will prepare to be a Papist."

us; in which wee were fully satisfied, y^t my Lett dated unto yo this day senight was to great a weight for Shaftesbury post to carry, for I sealed my lett with 2 seales and very fast in waxe. Under ye paper where it was sealed I then gott Mr. Richard Burge to deliver ye lett unto ye post master, by reason ffrankling sone is now an apprentice with him. But Mr. Bu: would warant this lett should goe safe. I told him not soe for two seales begetts a great jealosie & that blowinge this lett upp it would not be sealed againe; soe stands ye case and I thinke much ye better, for all ye heads of buishnesse in y^t lett followes

I there told you comeinge Thursday from Salisbury I mett with Mr. Mayor & my Brother Hur after some debate, they went downe unto Mr. Wittaker house, and came backe unto me againe, & then told me Mr. Witt would serve ye towne y^f they chused him freely, but noe randy nor pretence to any such thinge. I told you also how farr y^t would prvaile I knew not. I then told you y^t wee sent unto most part of ye masters, Mr. Murrell and about 30 more of our best and leadinge voyces & shewed yo lett unto them, or read it which I thinke was better. Upon our desires they made all ye rest of our freinds acquainted with yo: resolve, & ye next day most of them came unto me to Ned Willes & fully assured me y^t all your last voyces save but one stood most faithfully to you, and 12 new voyces added. I there told you also that our old Cosin Grove and his Sone sent there man unto me with full assurance of their freindes assistance, this beinge well considered, I confidently told you that noe one pson could stand in competion with you. Altho Mr. B's servant talked abroad in towne y^t 500*l.* was layd aside for ye good use of randy worke, & their agents Mr.

Windell & severall others was very early about towne & privately used all wayes & meanes but I suppose to litle purpose. And I thinke my letter which most likely fell open at post house by reason of two seales did noe harme at all. I like wise sayd yf any danger were possible to be foreseen it must be Sir And and Mr. B. to joyne togeather there may be some hazard. I hope wee are able to with stand that also, in a word I canot yet fore see but you are very safe. I have been at 5l. charge alreadie and y^t sume hath not been throwne away. Sir Matt Andrewes hath sent 3 lett to Mr. Mayor and offers to come downe, yf any good encouragment be returned but ye old bills must firs tbe payed my Bro Hu: lett dated this day unto you phapps will give you a more full account

S^r altho I written 3 times, to know whether the 15l. that Mr. Burge man ordered to be payd in unto Palmer was rec^d for I payd yo Bro Burye ye money, & have noe bill that Palmer rec^d it, pray doe not forgett itt to write me word, and you never answere one word about ye psentation of Chesleborne. Mr. ffreke told me you sayd some what to him about it doe as you please, but pray write me such a lett y^t I may shew unto him, I well know y^t Mr. ffreke will not be any way earnest to desire it unlesse you are very willinge to part with ye p^{r}sentn, but he will have some reason to thinke that I had not yo order to tell him that you were well pleased he should have it. I thinke on better tearmes you can never part with it.

S^r in your last written by Tom ffarr he told me of mony to be payd in by Starre unto Mr. Palmer. I have Palmer's recet for 58l. and payd Starre his mony, but I had sent you more mony before then I had of yor in my hands, soe that I tooke yeasterday fiftie eight pounds of Mr. Tho. Dibben, and pmised that Tom ffarr should pay his Bro ye like sume in London. Pray take care it may speedily be done. I am as weary of writeinge as you can be of reading

Vale
Yo obliged Unckell ye same whilst
WILL BENNETT

[No. 70.]

Shaftesbu Ffebr ye 6th 80

Deare Cosin

I have been in this towne ever since ffriday and Mr. Mayor my Bro. Hurman Mr Gray, Mr Murrell Mr. Butler myselfe, and 4 or 5 more have consulted all togeather about yo concerne, and at last I can give you a very uncertaine account. Mr. Napper is gone unto the Sheriffe for ye Writt: how soone he will returne wee knowe not, he was all over ye towne, gave very good wordes & spent about 10*l*. or 12*l*. but I thinke have prevayled but litle altho he reported many untruths about my Cosin Evans. All the towne of Shafton have been in great expectation of Mr Hyde Dinton comeinge to sett upp for a Burguesse, Mr. Sheane went as an embassador in ye name of 130 voyces to invite him unto towne and came home, sett all the bells a ringinge, and told many a good lye, 2 ginnyes for his paines I beeleve was one of them; but Mr. Hyde sent his man over to trye how ye people stood affected I thinke ye Mayor & Alderman dealt most faithfully with him, but many others desired his comeinge & I have good reason to beleeve were very earnest in it, & y^f

I take my measure right, both Mr. B and our Cosen Counssellor Matth^w Da: are the cheife actors in this designe Old Mr B came out of those parts yeasterday whether he was with Mr. Hyde or not, I know not, ye comon people of the towne expect Mr. Hyde to come tomorrow into Shafton, but I am not absolute of y^t opinion for this very reason; I went by my selfe about 8 of the clocke last night to honest Mr. ffrancklings house, and left my ffreindes at the Rose and Crowne, about 8 of the cheife I told Mr. ffranck: he and my selfe only togeather about my Lett stayinge 4 dayes to longe; 20 times at least he forswore that as wee drunke a pint of wine by ourselves, I asked him about Mr. Hyde comeing, and upon my request he shewed me Mr. Hyde lett: to him selfe, in which he desires his humble service unto Mr. B excused his comeinge y^t day, but will come very speedly, and pay his thankes unto Mr. B. and all his ffreindes whether he will come tomorow I canot judge; but I thinke he have very litle hopes at Hindon: yor ffreindes all advise for yo: speedie comeinge downe and we canot avoyd to water yo voyces tomorow altho it cost 10*l*. pray give yo full advice by the next.

Yo Unck: ye same
WILL BENNET.

[No. 71.]

Shaftesbury ffebr: ye 23/80

Deare Cosin

The pleasure Mr. Mayor my Bro Hurman my selfe & many more of yo ffaithfull freindes have had wthin this 16 dayes you canot imagine. Randyes upon randyes, all sorts of trecherous designes layd, to lessen yo interest in ye opinion of yor freindes, but your great enimyes in the towne, & beneath ye hill have missed their confident designes, for wee discovred their under ground mines, and countermines which would fill upp this sheet of paper to sett forth, but I have done about that, and am now come to our yeasterdays election.

S^r noe sooner was pclamation made but Mr. Henery Younge ye informer falls on Mr. Groves man in ye face of ye Court, & gave him severall blowes in ye face, of that more hereafter. We went on very fairely with ye poole and you had at the end thirteen scoare votes. Sr Matthew Andrew twelve scoare and Mr. Wittaker about eight scoare. Pclamation made psently in ye Court, Mr. Wittaker gave it for a losse wee psently went all to dinner togeather Mr. Witta Mr. Mayor his Brethren Mr. Boles son Mr. Still Capt Ffrye Mr. Maynard & many more, wee were very merry & freindly althogeather. About 4 a clocke in ye afternoon wee went downe unto ye hall & sealed ye indenture, as many of ye Comaltie joyned & witnessed it as would then. All are very well pleased: but ye tappe must keepe runninge daye and night, & this was not to be avoyded for our freindes must be pleased since they stood soe ffast after many temptations. I desire you to give me a Writt of ease, y^f you have more of this service to be done

Yo^r Unckell the same whilst

WILL BENNETT.

The Indenture is gone to Shreiffe this morninge

[No. 72.]

East Orchard March y[e] 3
[1680]

Deare Cosin,

I canot thinke mine dated y[e] 23 of ffebrary came unto yo: hand, in which I told you wee were very hard besett above hill & below y[e] hill, yet at last wee caryed y[e] day, without giveinge yo: great ffreinds y[e] trouble of beinge there; for Sir John Coventry Mr. ffreke and Mr. Thynn but the Satterday before y[e] election; pfered me to be there, yf I thought that wee were like to be worsted, & they were to here from me Sunday beinge y[e] next day, Mr. ffreke told me he would ride unto Dorcester Munday to election, & come home at night, & not goe next day unto y[e] election at Corfe, but I sent unto them that I hoped you were safe & I was not willinge to give them y[e] great trouble, nor add more charge then needs wee must, it is to much now, but had I followed y[e] advice of some of yo: ffreindes; it had abeen amost soe much more charge! I have rec[d] but 10*l.* as yet & that of ffarmer Blanford he have very litle more in his hands, & that 10*l.* I payd Hugh Ffrye, & have his acquittance S[e] Matth: And: ordered me to pay it as you directed, I have payd great part of y[e] expences with readie mony, as the beere was dranke I had y[e] great pleasure to be with yo: freindes to pay, & take part with them, for when I saw all trickes imaginable playinge, I resolved not to goe drove, yf it were possible to helpe it; I will pay all y[t] wee are engaged for the next weeke. Wee had done it this very day, but Mr. Napper sent me a lett last night; he could not meet me & so we appointed next weeke.

S^r I was at Shrowton yeasterday, & after I had fully satisfied my good master; how thinges went, as to every pticular, he is a very nice inquirer, he answered I am very glad Tom Bennett is chosen & begun yo: good health. But his great kindnesse, & generositie did not end there, he gave me tenn ginyes to give to ye poore in Shafton.

Besides Mr. ffreke gave me twentie ginyes more for me to spend on yo: ffreinds to drinke yo: good health, he doth not end his bountie, but told me that I must consider, & consult with my Shaftesbury freinds; how to lay forth one hundrede of poundes; that it may remaine to ye good of ye towne; and now I make use of his owne wordes, Mr. ffownes, Mr. Rowland Minnes and 3 or 4 gentle more pesent, he was pleased to say, I would not adone any of these thinges, had they neclected honest Tom: Bennett, and not a choose him.

Sir, I am to wayte on Mr. ffreke againe tomorow, but not at Shrowton I will then advise, (yf it be to my master good likeinge) to treat ye Alderman and their wifes with 3 or 4 ginyes, and wee will order ye rest of ye ginyes, to be spent in as decent & good order as possible, yf ye women drinke, & sippe a litle amongst ye men, or as they shall thinke fitt, never ye worse, your ffreindes increase in towne every day, wee had 24 voyces turned unto us ye day before ye election, there is noe man able to stand against you, yf there should be need againe, I hope you will grant my ffeet a writt of ease, for now all men are most fully satisfied I thinke, yf my great great tooes stand sound to me this springe I will neither charge head stomacke, nor ffeet, soe hard againe; phapps whilst I live; I thanke God I am well at p^{e}sent, but prettie warme with yeasterdayes worke, you never gave me a line in answere about Chesleborne p^{e}sentation, pray minde it in yo: next but doe as you please.

Yo: unckell the same
WILL BENNETT.

[No. 73.]

East Orch March the 21st 80

Deare Cosin

Yours of the 16th instant is now before mee: a Wenesday last Mr. Napper and I mett at Shafton, and that day and the next morninge we payd of our randy bills, my best way is to write noe more at p^{r}sent, for it is a trouble to me, that soe much mony should be so vainly spent, and you cannot judge it other wayes, then foolishly managed,

Mr. Napper had a 150*l*. brought him Tuesday night by Clarke the Caryer, and he told me, he had payd of almost all with readie money when he went twice over the towne, and Saint Ju: parish from house to house. I brought but 100℔ thinkinge that to be more mony a great deale then I had to pay, by reason I had payd 38℔ before with readie mony, 16℔ of it to my most exsactinge, & basely gripeinge Landlord Ned Willes for ye Election day: 7℔ for wine, when I gave him my full order to draw noe wine unlesse I was in ye roome. Nay he sent his Daughter unto mee at ye New Inn, whilst Mr. Whitta, Mr. Mayor his brethren & 20 more gentlemen at diner. I rose & went into ye galliry to her, shee told me her ffather sent her to let me know he had noe body to dine, & he desired leave to draw wine. I answered noe leave was to be given and I told him ye day before I did bespeake noe victualls: shee answered that shee was sorry to see her ffather soe used: when ye bill was called next morninge 30 ordinaryes, 7℔ in wine, sacke as his wife sayd, that pswaded people to drinke it, in good earnest it was not worth a groat a quart, & Ned told me of it fortnight before, altho they doe now confesse their base dealinge. I am goeinge to another house. I will now give you an account, how Mr. Napper & myselfe, found out waies to part with our mony: ffirst he would pay halfe a crowne for every voyce that voted for Sr Matthew for his diner, half a crowne between us had been much better: I allowed but fifteen pence for your halfe. I thinke they are much better pleased wth mee then with Mr. Napper, but Wensday about 7 of ye clocke Mr. Napper 150℔ was gone, and my 100℔ gone also, he had 60℔ more from Meere, I borowed 50℔ more of my Brother Hurman, & 10℔ I had in gold in my pockett. Mr. Napper payd away his last 60℔ & I payd away my 50℔ borowed, and my 10 ginyes (saved 3/6 to drinke) a 100℔ of this mony spent was beyound my order. My Cosin Evans had mault fitt to bee used at such a time, 50℔ worth of drinke in private houses, are yet to draw, they say they were bid to brew, I payd Old Stayner in bimport 3℔ and 6℔ more in two houses fast by, not Mr. Broadgate. in a word I thinke the voyces are all well pleased on our part, better much then on Sr Matth, but yo randy bills amounts to almost 200℔, payd 38℔ in Shaftesbury before Mr. Napper & I mett to pay togeather 100℔ brought from my house 50℔ more borowed that day 10 ginyes but 3/6 of this left that we spent. You canot be more troubled in readinge this letter then I was in my mind to pay itt, altho I durst not shew it to much, Mr. Napper payed more, better let that alone. I reced 20℔ of Collo Butler 10℔ of ffarmer

Blandford, I am promised 40℔ more of Collo Butler, Hugh ffrye receit for 10℔ so I have received but 20℔ as yet of the randy mony basely spent. Sir Matthew Andrew will give 10℔ a year for ever to a schoole master to teach poore boys to reade and write, to fitt to make apprentices [read on in the ffoote of Hugh ffryes acquittance.

[This acquittance is lost.]

[No. 74.]

S^r I heare you are prettie well as to ye gout but that ye relickes of yo: ffever remaines still with you, pray have a good heart, this is noe more then what is ye same, with all psons with us, that have had ye ffever, have but patience all will doe very well. Sir Andrewes is very kind to ye towne of Shafton he sendes downe ye votes every weeke to our Cosin Mr. Mayor it was moved by Mr. Mayor at towne Hall for a lett. of thankes to be returned to Sr Matth Andrewes, I think it was not fully agreed of y^e same.

    Yo Unckell & Servant
      WILL BENNETT.

[This is only a fragment of a letter.]

APPENDIX.

APPENDIX.

"August 28, 1675.

"Mr. Bennett,—I cannot but give you an account of the affair between me and my Lord Digby, it being come to that height to which my Lord Digby's ill-temper hath brought it. Mr. Hussy, whose mistake and natural good humour and particular kindness to me hath blown this coal, delivered me a letter from my Lord Digby to this effect: that upon the discourse of Colonel Strangways being made a Peer, who is just dead, the gentlemen of the country at the assizes had importuned him to serve as their Knight of the shire in his room, and desired my concurrence. I writ no answer neither then nor since to my Lord's letter; but in as civil terms as I could, and suitable to the respect I bore my Lord's quality and relatives, I told Mr. Hussy that the intimate friendship was between me and Mr. Freke would not permit me to give an answer until I knew his mind, for, if he stood, I and my little interest must certainly be for him. I saw not Mr. Hussy after that, until I met him in Guissage Street, where there passed no more words between us, I being in a coach and he on horseback, but that I told him Mr. Freke did not stand, and I knew no opposition to my Lord. The Saturday after, at the usual meeting at Blandford, the discourse amongst us was that my Lord Digby had nobody stood against him, but that we were all for him, as indeed I was at the time, but we neither obliged one another nor any of ourselves to my Lord or any of his agents that I know of, nor there was no one there that appeared to act on my Lord's behalf; so that all was mere discourse, and no obligation upon any, and you are my witness that I have no reason to be obliged, since I proposed both unto Sir William Portman at the hunting and to the company at Mr. Freke's afterwards, that we might send to my Lord Digby and the gentlemen of the West to give us a meeting at Blandford, and there unanimously and friendly agree on the election, which was not liked, and so I desisted. The day after that meeting at Blandford I had advice from a very good hand that my Lord Digby would not prove as some of us expected; upon which Mr. Whitaker doing me the favour to come over and dine with me, he may remember that I then told him I had great doubts concerning my Lord Digby and of the designs of some of our great men above, and the correspondence my Lord had with them. Upon this I sent to Mr. Browne of Frampton, to persuade him to stand, which he refused. Mr. Moore was then at Tunbridge Wells, and since his return myself and several of the gentlemen and freeholders of the county have prevailed with him to appear, but he declares that if Mr. Freke will yet please to stand, he will sit down and give his votes for him, for what he doth is merely for the service of the country; but I thought it an unreasonable thing to send to you or any other of my friends (with the advantage of time that my Lord Digby had without a competitor had pre-engaged) to ask your civility unto him, until I was sufficiently enabled to make appear how little he was like to answer those expectations you had of him, and what were the conditions of your being for him, but this my Lord hath sufficiently done to my hands; for meeting him yesterday by accident at Fernditch Lodge, before a great deal of company and ladies, he quarrelled with me for being against him, and told me that he was for the King and his country, and that I was against the King and for a commonwealth, and that he would have my head the next Parliament, and all this, notwithstanding I had met him some days before at Bowridge and told him that the reason I was not for him was that I was assured he was not for me, and that he had not dealt well with me to expect and seek my assistance whilst he kept a correspondence and was of the interest with some persons he well knew of; but my wife being then in the coach, I told him that whenever his Lordship would give me an honest discourse, I would sufficiently convince him that he had done me the injury in endeavouring to make ill use of me to serve that interest, and that otherwise I had that respect for him, being a nobleman, and that might be of so great use to the King's service and public interest, that I should ever desire to have all possible respect paid him by good men. Now, Mr. Bennett, judge you, if this be the case, as I have twenty witnesses, whether all honest men that love their country are not disengaged from their promise to him, nay rather, whether they are not obliged to oppose him, unless they mean his person and not the public interest. It is not my quarrel, for, as for what concerns me, I shall presently seek a public reparation. Sir, I have no more to say but that you will please to communicate this unto the rest of my friends.

"I am,

"Your very affectionate friend and Servant,

"SHAFTESBURY."

WYMAN AND SONS, PRINTERS,
GREAT QUEEN STREET, LINCOLN'S INN FIELDS,
LONDON, W.C.

www.ingramcontent.com/pod-product-compliance
Lightning Source LLC
Chambersburg PA
CBHW020829230426
43666CB00007B/1164